None of us can avoid pain and brokenness in this life – but there's a God who identifies with our suffering and has the power to free us from its chains. Our friend Jeannie lives with an inspiring confidence in the healing power of Jesus, and a huge passion to see broken lives restored in him. This wonderful book will bring hope and help to many.

Matt and Beth Redman
Worship leaders, authors and speakers

I couldn't put this book down. Fresh, unusual and insightful, Jeannie writes as she talks. She shows the reader how to move from hurting to healing using helpful illustrations from the lives of those she has prayed with over the years, as well as weaving in some moving stories of her own healing encounters with Jesus. It is worth every penny!

Mary Pytches
Author and international speaker

This is an extraordinary book. Full of great stories, helpful insights and biblical truth, it also inspires you to believe that things can be different and that change is possible. Jeannie then lays out practical steps to take on the road to freedom. This book is born out of years of hard thinking, extensive reading but most importantly compassionate, dedicated praying with people. I have had the privilege of praying with Jeannie for others (and for me!) over the last

20 years. She has managed to distil her love, faith and humour into this book. Genius.

David Westlake
Innovations Director at Tearfund and
Soul Action Director

Jeannie's book achieves so much. You cannot help to pick up her love for people. It is real, authentic, and you will meet Jeannie in its pages. But more than that, you will discover her Saviour, Friend and Lord, so that the release and freedom that she has experienced can become part of your life. I highly recommend this book for anyone who is living through these things, or working with those who are, as a practical, insightful and personal journey.

Roy Crowne
National Director, YFC

Let the Healing Begin

JEANNIE MORGAN

survivor

ISBN 978 184291 351 2

Survivor is an imprint of
KINGSWAY COMMUNICATIONS LTD
Lottbridge Drove, Eastbourne BN23 6NT, England.
Email: info@survivor.co.uk
Printed in the USA

I dedicate this book to the major loves of my life.
My husband Ken, you really are my 'other half'.
My daughters Sarah, Alex, Joanna and Beth.
I thank God that he made you all,
each one as precious as the other.

About the Author

Jeannie Morgan has been ministering to the broken-hearted for 25 years. She has been part of the Soul Survivor Watford Church leadership team since the church began and has a passion to see the church of all ages setting the captives free. During the last ten years she has travelled in the UK and abroad, training up youth groups and church congregations in both the healing ministry and leading workshops in ministry in the power of the Holy Spirit. Jeannie is a seminar speaker at the Soul Survivor national and international festivals.

Contents

With Thanks

I would like to thank all those at Soul Survivor Watford Church who encouraged me many times to write a book. Thank you, Mike Pilavachi, for listening to that 'inner voice' which prompted you to tell me to write a book and to 'hurry up and get on with it'.

More than anything, I would like to thank all those who allowed me to be present as they opened up their pain and grief to Jesus. At times the compassion of Jesus was strong; I felt his presence so close it was as if I could almost touch and smell him. Sometimes it was exquisite, like nothing else on earth. For all those who have allowed me to be present and a part of their healing journey, thank you.

I would like to thank those who have always encouraged and inspired me: Bishop David Pytches, Mary Pytches, David Parker, Nancy Parker, Rev. Barry Kissell, Rev. Margaret Knight, David Westlake, Liz Biddulph, Ruth Yule, Mike Pilavachi and Matt Redman. And of course my husband, Ken, who has always looked after me and supported me by being the 'breadwinner', enabling me to give my time to prayer ministry.

Thank you, Jesus, for what you have done, for what you are still doing, and for what you are going to do.

WITH THANKS

Foreword

Jeannie Morgan is one of the most remarkable people I have ever met. She has a ministry of counselling and healing that is amazingly fruitful and effective. I have noticed over the years that most people whose lives radiate the Lord Jesus to those around them and whose ministry leaves His imprint have been trained in the school of suffering. I think of Joseph, Moses, David and many of the prophets. Similarly, Jeannie's ministry began in tragedy. In the midst of her own pain and brokenness she encountered a living and loving God, and He healed her. He also put in her a burden to see others come to a place of wholeness in Christ and she has devoted herself to this cause ever since.

Jeannie has learned the secret of listening to Jesus and obeying what He says. The fruit over the years has been amazing. As I have served alongside Jeannie and her husband Ken – travelling the world together as well as serving in our local church, Soul Survivor Watford – I have lost count of the number of people whose lives have been permanently transformed when she has prayed for them. So often I have heard a commotion in a meeting, looked out and there has been Jeannie moving through the crowd like a little human dynamo, laying hands on anything that moved and leaving a wonderful trail in her wake. I am convinced that the reason Jeannie sees so much healing is because she is always pointing people to Jesus. She knows that it is only in a personal relationship with God that we find wholeness.

The lessons, principles and insights she has learned over the last 20 years of ministry are contained in this book. This is not a dry academic treatise on the healing ministry; it is an overflow of a life that is passionate in its pursuit of God and filled with His compassion for those who are broken and hurting. The stories and testimonies in this book are remarkable and authentic.

This is a hugely important book. The message is that we all can minister the healing of Jesus effectively. The insight and wisdom here will help you to do that. In an age when some seem to be moving away from a day-by-day dependence on the Holy Spirit and are instead relying on programmes and methods that begin with human ingenuity and effort, this book is a reminder that miracles happen when we depend on God and wait for Him to work. This book is a prophetic call to the church to 'do what the Father is doing'. It is a book of hope.

I commend this book wholeheartedly, because I can wholeheartedly commend both the author and the message. If you are longing to minister healing effectively, this wonderful book will give you many of the tools. If you are in pain and despair, this book will remind you that our God is the God who specialises in changing lives.

Mike Pilavachi
January 2007

FOREWORD

Introduction

It was a year after becoming a Christian that I first realised I was a sinner. To me at that time it seemed to be the least of my problems! First off, I met the Holy Spirit and he revealed Jesus the healer to me as I became a Christian from a time of great tragedy and saw my need of healing.

This book is both my story of how Jesus has brought his love and healing into my life, and the stories of many others to whom I have had the privilege of ministering the love of Jesus. My desire is to see the lost and broken being made whole and to be used as a channel and vessel of Jesus' healing love.

I hope that as you read these stories, illustrations and biblical accounts, you will stop reading, close your eyes and invite the Holy Spirit to come and unravel any pain from your past, and I pray that you will know a good measure of freedom.

Many of us have been hurt by events in our lives. The good news is that Jesus is very aware of what has happened to us in our past and he is aware of what is happening now. He is the same yesterday, today and for ever – we are not alone now, and we were not alone then. He is capable of giving us now what we didn't get in the past, so that we can go on with him in the future. Our heavenly Father sent the Holy Spirit not just into our churches: he is also available as a gift for *us* – our Counsellor and Comforter. He can come and visit us wherever we are, bringing the power of his love. Some of us have lost the art of allowing him to be our personal Counsellor and Comforter. Some of us never knew he could be such a thing.

This book is here for you to use as a tool, so that you can work through your pain over a period of time – doing the exercises, stopping and asking the Holy Spirit to come and minister to you – and make choices today that you didn't make in the past. Just reading this book will not heal you; it is very simple stuff, but if you invite the Holy Spirit to come, pray the prayers throughout each chapter, wait on him to show you things that happened in the past that affect you now, and invite the love of Jesus to come and heal you, then the potential for freedom and healing is enormous!

I am thankful to my Lord that he did not allow me to remain broken. I am a work in progress until finally I am with him for ever. Then I will be made complete and whole.

1: Taking Your Foot Off the Bottom of the Pool

Fold your arms, and look down. Which arm is on the top – the right or the left one? Now put your arms down and fold them again, but this time put the other arm on top. How does that feel? Say out loud what those feelings are. Are they any of the following: weird, uncomfortable, squirmy, strange? Well, for some of us that is how it will feel when Jesus starts to heal pain from the past. In the healing process this isn't a bad thing.

Another illustration of how the healing process feels sometimes, especially when you are choosing to change, is that it's a bit like vomiting. Do you remember a time when that happened to you? It's funny, isn't it, but those times are etched in our memories!

The times I can particularly remember are when I have woken in the middle of the night with a horrible feeling in my stomach. For about an hour I wrestle with the thought that I want to vomit. I try to think of something else, but this desire keeps getting stronger. It's like having a battle with a huge monster. I want to run away from it. I fight it. I would rather at that moment be anywhere else than where I am.

Suddenly I make the run to the toilet, my head is down the pan and I'm still fighting it – hoping that the toilet is clean! Suddenly, the point of no return, *hughieeeeee* (the pet name for it in our house) – it's up and out – my nose and throat are burning, my eyes are watering – I reach for a glass of water, my legs trembling.

The relief! Now I feel so proud of myself, so much better. I can't believe that I struggled and battled against it for so long. If only I'd realised earlier how much better I would feel.

Going through a time of healing can feel like all of the above. When a healing has taken place, you wonder why you resisted so much.

As you start to look at some of the issues you struggle with, it may well feel a bit like when you learned to swim. (Maybe you never did learn, but you'll still appreciate the elements in the illustration.)

I was 30 years old when I learned to swim. For years I pretended to swim in the shallow end of the pool. I didn't realise that people could actually see my legs through the water. One foot hopped along the bottom while the other one splashed. My head was bent back and my arms splashed about. I desperately wanted to 'fit in' with the rest of the people in the pool, but was too afraid to take my foot off the bottom and launch myself on top of the water.

LET THE HEALING BEGIN

One day, I made the choice: it was now or never. I put my will behind my decision and took my foot off the bottom. I trusted the water to take my weight. I was nervous, but excited too. I launched myself on top of the water, and to my surprise and delight it not only took my weight but gave me a wonderful sense of freedom. I was no longer restricted.

Making changes and receiving healing for past choices is a bit like that at times. Throughout this book there will be times when you feel just like you did when you first took your foot off the bottom of the pool. This is the moment of choosing with your mind – using your will to say 'yes' and trusting that God is big enough to uphold you and carry you through.

With these three different illustrations held in mind for future reference, let's continue: together let's start the journey of receiving healing for our past hurts.

Let's pray
(Either read this and say it in your own words, or say this prayer out loud.)

Jesus, I so want to get healed up. I don't want to live my life like this any more. Please come, Holy Spirit, and enable me to open up to you. Take me on this journey of healing. I surrender myself to you now and allow you access to my past. Amen.

Now just be still, shut your eyes for a couple of minutes and receive the power and person of the Holy Spirit. This isn't about a feeling: it's about inviting what the Bible calls 'the power from on high' to come and be present. Whenever you start to read a section of this book, just take a couple of minutes to say this type of prayer.

Most of the church is made up of the walking wounded. That is how some of us came to be Christians in the first place: we needed Christ the healer. That is what happened to me.

I was brought up in a loving, but in some ways dysfunctional family (later on I will reveal more about that). Neither of my parents were Christians. My mum had attended a Catholic school as a child, and my dad's mother was a clairvoyant and my dad held spiritualist beliefs. For some reason they decided that I should attend a Church of England Sunday school. The only things I remember being taught at Sunday school were that when crossing the road I should make the sign of a cross on my chest in case I was run over, and that if I told lies I would get black spots on my heart! I knew I had at least two spots already and used to get worried that they might spread. Armed with this very useful theology, I embarked on the rest of my life.

When I was 16 years old, I met Ken at my place of work. He was three years older than me, so waited until I was 17 to ask me out. By the time I was 18 we were engaged, and we married when I was 19. We were happy and after a couple of years decided to start a family. Unknown to me, the baby I was carrying had a severe deformity. In fact, her brain hadn't developed at all, so she was unable to sustain life and was stillborn when I was 36 weeks pregnant. This was such a terrible blow to us. I felt as if I didn't belong with my friends who did have children, and I felt different from those friends who didn't have children. I felt as if I had fallen between these two groups into a no-man's-land. As well as feeling very different, I felt enormously guilty. I had done nothing wrong, but this feeling hung over me. I had looked forward to and planned activities and events for our child's life way ahead into the future. I'd imagined her at the school around the corner, playing with other friends' children. Suddenly that was not to be. I became extremely angry with God. That was strange, as I'd never 'known' him. I remember one day shouting out at him, 'I never ever want to know you!' It's astonishing to me now that I said that, as I didn't realise at the time that it *was* possible to 'know God'.

I sank into a place of darkness and loneliness. Within three months I was pregnant again. This time I was determined not to get caught out. I was determined not to build up any relationship with the child growing inside me. I didn't talk to this little baby, or tell her anything about her family. This baby was a total stranger who just fed off me. When I was 36 weeks pregnant I was given an X-ray (in those days scans were not available at my local hospital). I remember the consultant coming to the side of the couch and saying, 'Mrs Morgan, I'm pleased to tell you that everything is fine – the shape of your baby's head is just as it should be.'

I burst into tears. 'I'm pregnant, I'm pregnant!' was all I could repeat.

'Yes,' the consultant said condescendingly, 'we can see that.'

He didn't understand that from that moment, I allowed myself to believe that I was going to have a baby, one who had the ability to live outside the womb. For the next four weeks I was elated. When Alexandra was born I was ecstatic. Everyone on duty knew I had given birth to her. Whenever anyone passed the door I would say, 'I've just had a beautiful little girl – her name is Alexandra!'

'Yes we know,' they would reply. 'Everyone knows; the whole hospital knows!'

I was so excited I didn't sleep that night for longer than an hour. This continued for the next ten days while I was in hospital – just one hour's sleep each night. When I came out of there, I was in a very unstable condition. I ended up running up and down the stairs naked and screaming one night and was put to bed, where I went into the foetal position and sucked my thumb. I was in such a state that I couldn't even say whether I wanted a hot drink or a cold drink. For three more weeks I only had one hour's sleep a night. For six weeks I was unable to make any decisions or care for our little baby. In all, the depression was with me for three months.

I had a fantastic doctor (I later discovered he was a Christian). He visited me every day during those first three weeks, even though he was on his vacation. The night before he was due to commit me to a psychiatric hospital, I sat up all night in bed and somehow the shock of leaving again all that was familiar to me was like being plunged into an icy cold bath. My sanity was restored. When the doctor came to take me to hospital the next day, I had recovered my mind enough to speak to him. I didn't know it at the time, but he had asked a Christian prayer group to pray for me. I now know that their prayers were answered. Over the next few months, I slowly recovered from that deep depression and went on a course of relaxation classes that really helped me.

After a couple of years, we decided to have another child. Joanna was beautiful too. Blonde and curly. When she was two years and three months old, tragedy struck. As I was answering the front door to Alexandra, unknown to me Joanna had run back outside to the garden. She fell into the swimming pool. Later we realised she must have chased one of our cats outside. It probably had a bird in its mouth, as we later found a dead bird on the kitchen floor. Joanna hated the pool as it wasn't heated, and she didn't usually go near it. We thought she was upstairs, but as Alex and I reached the half-landing and looked outside, we saw Joanna floating in the pool.

I sent Alex next door to a neighbour and carried Joanna along the street, screaming for help. I laid her on the ground and gave her mouth-to-mouth resuscitation as best I could. The ambulance arrived and we were taken to the accident and emergency department of the local hospital. I was taken into a relatives' room and a nurse waited with me while they worked on Joanna. I turned to the nurse and said, 'God is punishing me again – he did that to me before with my other baby.'

She put her big arms around me and hugged me, saying in her rich Afro-Caribbean accent, 'Honey, our God doesn't work like that.'

What she said to me was truth, and it entered me and immediately took hold of that lie inside me. At that moment I knew that what I had said wasn't true.

It was such a frightening time. When two doctors came into the room, I backed off towards the window, wanting to jump out of it. They said it was possible that either Joanna would be like a vegetable all her life, or she would have no brain activity at all and she would die. At that moment, I prayed my first prayer since I was a child, and I prayed that she would die. I couldn't bear the thought of watching her every day, lifeless. She was such a gentle, beautiful little girl. By this time, my husband Ken had arrived and we were told that it might be a few days before they knew anything more and that it would be best for us to go home. They would contact us if anything changed. We went home and the doctor sedated me so that I could sleep.

The following morning we had a phone call to say that Joanna had died. Obviously this is just an outline of what happened and there is a lot more to this story, but I want to tell you more later.

The reason why I felt God had punished me was that I had decided to have an operation to be sterilised the year before, because of medical reasons. I was confident then that I would never want to have any more children. Now this fact just screamed at me. My arms felt so empty. It felt as if I'd had part of my body amputated. Joanna had been with me most of the time – like an extension of myself. My thoughts all day were: Where is she? Is she safe? What is she doing? Now nothing. I couldn't bear to see our other daughter Alex suffering so much pain. She missed her sister so much. They were like twins, although there were three years between them. If Joanna fell and hurt herself, Alex would cry. She couldn't bear to see her hurt. In fact,

LET THE HEALING BEGIN

they were so close that they had given up sleeping in separate rooms so that they could see each other as soon as they woke in the morning.

After Joanna died we had lots of visits from David Pytches, the local vicar, and Barry Kissell from St Andrew's Church in Chorleywood.

David said some comforting things and, one day, as we stood in the kitchen with him just before he left, he asked if he could pray. He then did a very strange thing and asked Jesus to come into our kitchen with his love and power. What a weird thing, I thought: isn't Jesus at churches – not in kitchens?

As David left, I said to him, 'For a vicar I think you're a very nice person, but I really don't want anything you have on offer.'

However, the strangest thing was that every time I went into the kitchen after that, I sensed a warmth not present anywhere else in the house. I also started to have a sense of hands drawing me along. It was if they were beckoning me on a journey. If anyone at that time had told me about the Holy Spirit and described what he did, I would have said, 'Oh yes, I know him.' I started to have many other experiences that were both good and supernatural. Maybe I'll have to write another book about that!

A couple of months later, I was talking to an acquaintance, a nurse called Debbie who was married to a surgeon. She said to me, 'Have you ever thought of having a reversal of your sterilisation operation?'

'No,' I said, 'but I'm having a think about it now!'

Later on Debbie said to a mutual friend, 'I don't know why I said that to Jeannie about the operation – my husband said obstetricians are butchers at fine operations like that.'

In fact, in England the success rate for reversal of sterilisation operations was only 10 per cent. The following week, I had dropped Alex off at school and was walking back home when I heard a voice in my head. The only way I can describe it is as very big, very deep and very warm. The voice said, 'Trust in me, trust in me, trust in me.' The next moment, I heard another voice, very whiney, just like the voice of the serpent in the *Jungle Book* film, saying, 'Trust in me, trust in me.' At that time I didn't realise that the serpent was a significant beast, as I had never read the Bible. I made a big decision: I didn't want in any way to trust the serpent voice – it sounded horrible. At the same moment as deciding I wanted the warm, deep voice, I had an incredible urge to run home and telephone the consultant who had done the sterilisation operation.

First of all, I rang Ken and told him what I wanted to do. He sounded worried, as he didn't want me to get my hopes up. After that I rang and made an appointment with the consultant. Then, for the first time since I was a little child, I got down on my knees to pray. For some reason I went into the bathroom and knelt by the sink. 'Please God, give me a baby. Amen.' I knew no other way to pray than to speak back to that big, warm voice that had been in my head.

When Ken and I went to see the consultant, he had some amazing news. He had been pioneering a new method of reversing sterilisations. He said that he had a 75 per cent success rate. (What he didn't tell us until a year later was that he had only done four of these operations, of which three had worked! The last time he had done this operation was a year previously.) Hope swelled up inside me. This was the first time in months that I had felt such a thing.

Three months after the reversal operation, I became pregnant with another little girl, whom we named Elizabeth. Three weeks after she was born we were told that her name means 'a gift from God'.

David the vicar continued to call and one day left me a Bible. To be polite, I thought I had better read a bit before he came back. The first part I read was Ecclesiastes. I found it so amazing. This man was describing things that I felt. He had a lot of negative thoughts, was pessimistic and sometimes sounded depressed and in despair. Somehow it felt comforting to find someone who thought and felt this way too! When David came back for a visit, I was enthusiastic as I told him what I had been reading. 'Goodness me!' he said. 'There are much better things to read in the Bible than that.'

I told him how worried I was about Joanna, as she hadn't been christened as a baby. We hadn't wanted to be hypocritical, as we weren't believers, but now I didn't know where she was. Was she in heaven?

David replied, 'It says in the Bible that if you are as a little child you will enter the kingdom of heaven, and also Jesus said, "Let the little children come to me and do not stop them, for the kingdom of heaven belongs to such as these."'

At first I found this very comforting, and then after a couple of days I started to feel restless, as I realised that if

Joanna was in heaven . . . what about me? How was I going to get there too?

I decided that it was time I paid for the Bible David had given me. I had been brought up proudly, although we had been poor, and was always taught to pay for what I had been given and not to accept charity. So I went to my first service at St Andrew's, as I didn't know any other way to contact David Pytches, to pay for the Bible. As I sat in the church, I felt as if I was enfolded in cotton wool. This is the only way I can describe it. I wasn't sure what it was I was feeling. I felt safe and I was experiencing something for which I had no words. Later I realised that the 'cotton wool' was in fact love that people were expressing to Jesus and the safety and security of being amongst the body of Christ.

For three months after Joanna died I could not grieve or cry. But, as I sat in that church, I felt grief rising. This became my place to cry. It felt like a safe place. No one interfered. I sometimes felt a hand on my shoulder as I wept. I went up for communion – fortunately no one told me that you had to be a Christian or a believer to receive it! It was as if layers of grief were coming off me.

For three consecutive weeks someone preached an evangelistic sermon at church with an invitation to receive Jesus. For each of these weeks I prayed and asked Jesus to come into my life. At the end of the three weeks I thought, 'This is ridiculous. I can't keep on doing this – either this Jesus is the truth, or it's all a lie.' Up until this point I had always thought of Jesus as a fictional figure, the Bible a fairy story. This was now the time to make a choice. I decided to take the step of trusting that Jesus was the truth and not a lie.

LET THE HEALING BEGIN

Nothing happened that day, but the next day when I woke up everything seemed to be in focus. It was like the first time I wore my glasses. I didn't know that I had been looking at everything through blurry lenses. It was only when I could see clearly that I realised what I had been missing.

Everything in creation looked different now. It was like an awakening to clarity. I also started to allow Jesus to come and share my grief. I started to let the Holy Spirit be the Comforter and Counsellor in my life. The healing had started.

Let's pray

Jesus, I thank you for your healing power. I want to know you as my Healer. I want to receive you as my Healer now. Thank you that you want to bring me freedom and healing in my life. However you want to do it, I am willing. Amen.

More of my story will unfold as we start looking at specific areas of pain.

After seeing so much healing in my own life, I have had a *big passion* both to see others receive this same freedom and to enable others to set the captives free.

Obviously Jesus has a much bigger passion than mine, and he is the model to look to.

We see Jesus in the Bible setting free the physically afflicted, the emotionally sick, those who are mentally ill and those troubled by evil spirits.

In Isaiah 61 we read:

The Spirit of the Sovereign LORD is on me,
    because the LORD has anointed me
    to preach good news to the poor.
He has sent me to bind up the broken-hearted,
    to proclaim freedom for the captives
    and release from darkness for the prisoners,
to proclaim the year of the LORD's favour
    and the day of vengeance of our God,
to comfort all who mourn,
    and provide for those who grieve in Zion –
to bestow on them a crown of beauty
    instead of ashes,
the oil of gladness
    instead of mourning,
and a garment of praise
    instead of a spirit of despair.
They will be called oaks of righteousness,
    a planting of the LORD
    for the display of his splendour. (Isaiah 61:1–3)

Although this is written in the Old Testament, it was a prophecy about what Jesus was coming to do. Jesus himself read out this same scripture in the temple (Luke 4:16–19). He had just been tempted by the devil for 40 days in the desert. He read this out as his manifesto, a bit like politicians do now, the difference being that Jesus actually did what he said he was going to do!

After reading out that scripture from Isaiah, Jesus said, 'Today this scripture is fulfilled in your hearing.' He said that this was what he was coming to do – to bring freedom, healing, forgiveness, restoration, *then and now*.

Jesus didn't just walk about with his hands in the air and everywhere he walked people got healed. People actually came to him. Some people he gave instructions to.

Some people had to do something to enable the healing to happen or to receive their healing.

In healing and receiving freedom from past hurts, we usually have to *do something*. It doesn't just happen; it's an active process, not a passive one.

On this healing journey, we will be actively coming to Jesus. We will need to take steps and make choices. Sometimes this will mean reversing the choices we made in the past. It may be that we have to choose with our mind and will to reverse something that we decided years ago.

Sometimes it will involve repentance – which means turning away from something that is a pattern of behaviour or sin. Repentance is active, like forgiveness.

It's about allowing Jesus – the one who is the same yesterday, today and for ever – to come and visit those locked-up emotions.

It's about allowing him to come and bring his healing touch to those past hurts.

It's about learning about the nature of God, coming to an understanding of who we are in him.

It's about wholeness of body, mind and spirit.

In Matthew 5:48 Jesus said, 'Be perfect . . . as your heavenly Father is perfect.' Sounds like a tall order! The word 'perfect' doesn't mean moral perfection here. It means wholeness. It means completeness, wholeness for our body, mind and spirit. It means be whole as your heavenly Father is whole.

We will never be completely whole in this life – not until we get to heaven – but, by getting rid of stumbling blocks on our journey, we can become more whole.

One illustration of this in the Old Testament (Jeremiah) describes a potter and his clay. The potter trims off excess clay. The clay starts off as a shapeless lump, but then is moulded into something beautiful. Another good illustration, this time from the New Testament, is that of God as the Gardener, pruning branches that don't produce fruit. That's what he wants to do with us: he wants to get rid of the bits that are dead or surplus or unproductive, things that are sinful, unhealthy or unclean.

We can see that wholeness involves our body, mind and spirit. The 'whole' of us is affected when we have painful episodes in our life. At first we use survival strategies, and as we grow older we use coping strategies to suppress our pain. Read Mary Pytches' book *Dying to Change*. Some of these coping strategies may involve any of the following:

- eating disorders: bulimia, compulsive eating, or anorexia
- self-harm: drug or alcohol abuse, cutting or hitting ourselves
- money: spending sprees, gambling
- sex: being promiscuous, having affairs
- fantasy: daydreaming, avoidance
- depression: withdrawing

Add your own coping strategies to this list. . .

The question to ask ourselves is, 'Are these coping strategies working?' Maybe they do for an hour or two, but then the cycle starts again.

For some of us, our spirit got crushed by bad things happening to us when we were young. Our body can sin or be sinned against. Our mind can feel tortured by others. People came to Jesus with all these things and more.

LET THE HEALING BEGIN

We need to get into the habit of *coming to Jesus*, not waiting to see if he will come to us.

Some people who came to Jesus were given instructions (see John 9:1; Luke 19:2; Mark 2:4; 1:40).

- The man born blind from birth was told to wash his eyes in the river.
- Zacchaeus had to get down from the tree.
- The paralysed man had to take up his mat and walk.
- The man with leprosy had to go and show himself to the priest.

If we want freedom from past hurts, we have to do something. It doesn't just happen.

On two occasions Jesus asked a blind man, 'What do you want me to do for you?' Was that a joke? Wasn't it obvious what the man wanted? (See Luke 18:41; Mark 10:51.)

These accounts show us that Jesus wants us to be specific when we seek healing, otherwise how will we know if healing is happening or not? How will God get the glory for it if we're not specifically asking and then seeing it happen?

Jesus is asking you today, 'What do you want me to do for you?'

Choose either of the following ways to pray, depending on whether you are a visual person or not:

(1) We can use our imagination to pray

We can turn our imagination over to the Holy Spirit and he can use it to bring the healing of Jesus.

Let's pray

Please come now, Holy Spirit, into my imagination – I open it up to you, Jesus.

See yourself in a room, a room in which you feel safe. Look for the door in the room. In Revelation Jesus says, 'I stand at the door and knock. If anyone . . . opens the door, I will come in and eat with him' (3:20). This means that Jesus wants to come in and share an intimate time with you, to be close. Just go to the door and open it. He wants to come in. Just like the people in the Bible, tell Jesus what you want him to do for you. Be specific; tell him that you are opening yourself up to him. Take a step of trusting what you can't see. Allow Jesus to do what he wants.

Take time to wait on him now and trust him.

(2) For those of us who are not visual in prayer

Let's pray

Please come, Holy Spirit; I open myself up to you, Jesus. You say in your Word that you want to come in and spend time with me. I choose now, as far as I am able, to open up to you. Come into every part of me. Just as the people asked you in the Bible, I want to ask you now specifically to do some things for me. Specific areas of my life need healing. I look to you now and trust you to show me in the weeks ahead the different ways you are going to bring that about. Thank you, Lord, for what you are going to do. Amen.

LET THE HEALING BEGIN

Some of us will know that something significant happened when we prayed that prayer. Others will feel that not much seemed to happen. Whichever group you fall into, the important thing to remember is that we need to be specific in prayer.

Healing is a gradual process. When it is instant, it is called a miracle. If we break a leg, it doesn't heal overnight. The process of healing from past hurts also takes time. It involves a renewing of our mind, a choosing with our mind and will to reverse things that we chose to believe in the past. Maybe we chose to believe that we were stupid. Maybe we believed that we were unlovable. We need to confess the sin of doing that and turn away from the negative thoughts. We need to give and receive forgiveness; we need to let Jesus into our past pain and allow it to be expressed. And of course we need to know more about the nature of God. Throughout the rest of the book I will show how some of this can happen.

GUILT AND FALSE GUILT
Isaiah 61 (see the quote on p. 28) speaks of captives and prisoners: freedom for captives and release for prisoners.

Prisoners have usually done something wrong, which is why they are imprisoned. They are often in a dark place, unable to see beyond the prison. They are suffering the consequences of their actions. When they have served their time, they are released, or else they are pardoned and set free.

Captives have usually been taken against their will, and have had something done to them: they may have been tied up, for example.

Let's look at where we have caused ourselves to be a prisoner, or where we could have been made captive in our past.

We can be prisoners of our sin – our wrongdoing. We may ask for forgiveness, but often we do not know how to receive forgiveness.

Sometimes as children we can learn to react in a certain way; it becomes a pattern and we are unaware of when it started. One day in church I realised that the significance of what Jesus did on the cross for me didn't seem to impact me. It wasn't that I thought I never did anything wrong. It was more to do with the fact that if I said sorry, I had no expectation of anything changing. I asked Jesus why this was, and I had a revelation of how my past had caused a pattern of reaction regarding asking for forgiveness.

When I was a child, my mother suffered almost constant depression and was a chronic/acute agoraphobic (she didn't go out and had a phobia of outside space). Because of her mental state, she was always taking to her bed for days at a time. I used to get into trouble for minor things and would be summoned to the bedroom to say 'sorry'. I remember standing by her bed many times, saying 'sorry' for something that seemed so insignificant. Then nothing. I wasn't told that I was forgiven, or that everything was now OK. Not only did it make me feel rejected, but there seemed to be no point in saying 'sorry'. The relationship was not restored or reconciled. Nothing changed. I had humbled myself, and sometimes my only feelings were of humiliation as some of the things I was supposed to have done wrong were blown up out of all proportion in my mother's depressed mind.

When I became a Christian and asked for forgiveness, my expectation was the same as when I was a child. I had no expectation of being forgiven. It meant nothing to me. Nothing happened in the past when I said 'sorry', so why should it be any different now? My past had affected my present.

After a while, I learned that Jesus is nothing like my mother. He forgives and forgets my sin when I say 'sorry'. It says in the Bible that he will remember it no more. Another verse says it's as if it's thrown into the furthest part of the sea. What Jesus did on the cross was so powerful that not only was I forgiven, but I was also cleansed of my wrongdoing.

Our sin can make us emotionally and physically sick and can affect us even when we try and worship God. The following story illustrates this.

I was on an international Soul Survivor trip and prayed with a guy who was very troubled. I'll call him Michael. As I started to pray for him, his arms went rigid and were raised above his head. He was crying out in pain. No matter what I prayed, his arms would not move. I asked him if this had ever happened to him before. 'Yes,' he said. 'Only when I worship God.' This seemed really odd to me, as obviously God loves us to worship him – he doesn't usually give us pain when we do it! I asked all the obvious questions, like 'Have you ever been involved in the occult in any form?', but nothing provided an answer. Then I felt prompted by the Holy Spirit to ask him, 'Has anything happened in your life recently?' In reply, Michael told me that he had become a Christian three months earlier and that his dad had died recently. He started to cry as he thought about his dad, and was crying out with pain in his arms.

Things were hotting up in the auditorium where we were sitting. The band had come on stage and were tuning up for the evening gig. With the help of another person, I got Michael to stand up and walk out into another room – still with his arms stretched high above his head. To make him feel less embarrassed, I said to him, 'At least you'll never see any of these people ever again.'

'Oh yes I will,' he replied. 'This is my school.' Oops!

When we were sitting down in the other room, a question popped into my head. 'Before you became a Christian,' I asked, 'who meant the most to you in life? Who was your hero or idol?'

Immediately he burst out with, 'My dad, my dad was my idol, I worshipped him!'

That was it. Of course it was OK to grieve and mourn the loss of his dad – it was a huge thing, but what he was doing was sin. Michael idolised his dad. He had made him into an idol to be worshipped. God said that we must have no other gods besides him. It was and is a command. All Michael had to do was confess his sin to God and receive forgiveness. Immediately after he received forgiveness, he was able to move his painful arms – they were completely normal. It all happened very fast.

This was an amazing illustration to me of how sin affects our body. It was demonstrated in a way neither Michael nor I will ever forget.

Another time, also abroad, I prayed with a girl I'll call Mary. She really wanted to be married. She told me a bit about her past. Every time she told someone her story, they wanted to cast evil spirits out of her. She lived in a country where there seemed to be a habit of casting demons out of everyone for everything, even if they just had a common cold! The result for Mary was that it had caused her to feel very confused and unwell most of the time. In fact, she was only working part time as she couldn't concentrate on her job. She wondered how many more evil spirits she must have. After listening to the things she was struggling with, it seemed obvious to me that her problems boiled down to plain old ugly sin, not evil spirits. Having pointed out what they were, I suggested that she needed to confess her sins, receive forgiveness from Jesus and allow his love to enfold her. Her confession would also need to involve repentance. This is more than just saying 'sorry': it's about choosing to turn away from that pattern of wrongdoing and choosing to face Jesus instead. This she did. After this her face and body language looked transformed. Her mind felt clear. Three months later, I heard that she was getting married and had a new job working full time.

Psalm 38 speaks of sin and the way it can cause sickness in the body.

Jesus healed a paralysed man who came through the roof on a mat lowered by his friends. First of all, Jesus forgave the man his sin, then he healed him.

When we keep confessing the same sin, but don't turn away from it, or when we don't receive the forgiveness Jesus offers us, the Bible says that 'the wages of sin is death'. Our sin can cause us to feel guilty, and guilt is like a death: it cripples and binds us, it eats away at us, trying to destroy us. Satan is the enemy of Christians and he loves us to feel guilty. There is no freedom for us when we feel guilty. Psychologists say that the people who suffer the most from guilt are Christians. How strange, when we are the people who have been saved! Jesus became the guilt offering for us. He paid the 'wages of sin' for us by dying on the cross.

The disciple Peter disowned Jesus three times after Jesus was arrested. When he realised what he had done, Peter wept bitterly. He was sorry, but more than that, he repented – he did something, he turned away from that wrongdoing.

I have to live with the consequences of my actions, but I don't have to live with my guilt.

After our daughter Joanna drowned, I lived with a lot of guilt. Sometimes I would feel overwhelmed by it. My job was to look after my little girl, and I had failed to keep her safe. The swimming pool was old and had a net that covered it most of the time. It took two of us to fix the net in place, and we had used the pool at the weekend but hadn't replaced the net. In my view, I should have insisted we covered the pool immediately, instead of relying on the fact that Joanna hated to go in the water because it was unheated. I would go over and over the scene in my head, blaming myself and feeling guilty about what had happened. I also thought that Ken blamed me. He never said so, but I was too scared to ask him if he felt that way.

One day I was doing some ironing and had a teaching tape on (by this time I was a very new Christian). At the same time as listening, I was also praying, saying 'sorry' to Jesus for not being a good parent and for not being there when Joanna drowned in the pool. At that moment the voice from the tape said, 'If you keep saying "sorry" to Jesus and do not receive forgiveness, it's like saying that what Jesus did for you on the cross was not enough to forgive your sins.' This was amazing to me. I certainly didn't want to do that! I started again to say, 'Sorry, Jesus. . .' and then started to laugh as I saw that I was doing it again! Jesus did forgive me. What I was not doing was forgiving myself. I realised that I had to forgive myself and give my guilt to Jesus. That was where I was stuck. I carried my guilt around with me as if it were my punishment.

What a relief I felt! I was forgiven. I didn't need to carry that guilt any more. My Jesus, my Lord, carried it for me – he wanted to. That's what his love is like.

After a while, I realised that none of us can save our children. If I held Joanna's hand every minute of the day, trying to protect her, I still couldn't save her. We could have been walking along the road and a car could have mounted the pavement and killed her. I had to let all my guilt go.

If I hadn't forgiven myself, it would have been like saying to Jesus, 'Your forgiveness isn't enough.' That would be me putting myself above Jesus. That is sinful. Not to forgive myself is sinful. It is putting my standards above God's standards. So let's get rid of sin and experience freedom.

Have you a stick that you hit yourself with, things you have done or things you have not done? Do you blame yourself or feel guilty?

Jesus became the guilt offering for us on the cross. That's where we need to bring our guilt, to the cross.

Let's pray

Jesus, I want to be free of the hook of guilt. I want to be free now. Jesus, I come before the cross, the place where you went so that I could be free. (See yourself at the cross with Jesus, or think of the Bible story of Jesus on the cross.) *I am sorry that I have blamed myself. I am sorry that I haven't received your forgiveness. I want to do that now. I choose to let go of my guilt. I choose to let go of the ways in which I have blamed myself. I repent of that and choose to turn away from it now. In your name, Jesus, I choose to forgive myself. I thank you that you forgive me. I choose to receive that forgiveness. Thank you that you love me and forgive me. Thank you that you keep no record of wrongs. You said on the cross, 'It is finished.' Thank you, Lord. Amen.*

In the weeks ahead, look out for the times when you are blaming yourself. Immediately choose not to. Start breaking the habit. When things happen that make you feel guilty, pray again to be free until this becomes such a habit that you no longer take guilt upon yourself.

We can grow up in a family that constantly criticises us, that has unattainable standards. Then we can go through life trying to attain that standard, but constantly failing. We might not realise that we have adopted this standard as being the right and good thing to do, but in fact it could change us into being a workaholic or a perfectionist. Or we can have a habit of never feeling pleased with anything we achieve, always feeling inferior to others. Or else we could become a people-pleaser to earn a reward, the joker in the crowd. As children we learn to act in ways that bring praise and avoid punishment. This can become a pattern in our lives.

My mum was a perfectionist. If I bought her a present for her birthday or at Christmas, it was never right. Her reaction would be, 'Oh, what a shame it's not blue,' or, 'Mmm, that's a bit bigger than I expected,' or, 'Didn't they have something thicker/thinner?' It took me 35 years to realise that I would never please her. It wasn't possible, even if I spent a lifetime trying. The good news is that I stopped trying, which was a lot better for me! What a relief! I let the guilt go.

Whose standard do you want to aspire to – your family's standard, or Jesus' standard?

We need to recognise where this pressure comes from and bring it to the cross. Only Jesus is perfect. No other person is. He knows we are imperfect, fallen, helpless and weak. But he loves us anyway, in spite of this. It doesn't stop him using us or loving us. He hates the sin, but loves the sinner.

We need to give up what was put upon us by our family.

Let's pray
Holy Spirit, please come. (See Jesus at the cross.) *Jesus, I bring to you my family and their expectations of me. I lay down before you their high standards for me. I choose now in your name, Jesus, to let go of their standards of perfectionism, and of that desire always to please them even when it was unattainable. I choose to please you and to be free of this guilt now. Amen.* (If this has reminded you of any other guilt, bring that to Jesus as well.)

TAKING YOUR FOOT OFF THE BOTTOM OF THE POOL

Guilt happened in the world soon after the beginning of creation. Adam and Eve had no knowledge of good and evil – they had no sense of guilt. As soon as Adam and Eve sinned, however, they suddenly realised they were naked and they hid away from God. That's what guilt does: it keeps us away from God.

Satan tempted Eve then and he tempts us in the same way today. He wants to see us burdened by guilt. Why? Because it keeps us away from God and puts a barrier there. God saw that they were ashamed; *they* saw that they were naked. What did God do? He clothed their nakedness with clothes made of animal skin. They still had to live with the consequences of their sin, but they didn't have to live with their shame.

Sometimes we think we let God down. We can't possibly do that. He is almighty God, God Almighty. How could *we* possibly let *him* down? Look at us!

In the Bible we are told that Zacchaeus was a little man. He cheated people out of their money. His guilt made him hide up a tree to see Jesus. He obviously didn't have any friends to lift him up onto their shoulders. He was lonely because he was a cheat – he probably felt guilty because he had done wrong. Jesus saw him up the tree and immediately accepted him, sin and all. Jesus called up to him, 'I'm coming to your house for tea.' The acceptance and forgiveness from Jesus made Zacchaeus change. He gave back all the money to the people he had cheated.

Guilt affects our relationships. It makes us blame others and shifts the blame from ourselves. It can lead to depression.

Guilt can affect our body: it can weaken it and become

LET THE HEALING BEGIN

a self-punishment. Depression can be an easier thing for us to bear than the burden of facing our guilt. After the birth of my second child Alexandra, I was suicidal for a while during the depression. I felt guilty about the fact that my first baby had been deformed. I felt responsible for causing her to be like that. Maybe I hadn't eaten the right foods. Maybe I couldn't be trusted to look after Alex properly. What if I did it wrong? I switched off so that I was incapable of looking after her. She would be someone else's responsibility, and then I couldn't get the blame. This wasn't something I thought through: it just happened.

Grief can also cause us feelings of guilt. If someone dies because of a terminal illness, we can think that we should have seen the signs earlier and done something to prevent it.

Our guilt can also cause fear. It was years before I plucked up courage to ask Ken if he blamed me for Joanna drowning. During arguments, fear would rear its head. Deep down, I thought he blamed me – but I never asked him, because I was too afraid of the answer. When I did ask him, he said, 'Of course I don't blame you. It took two people to put the safety net on, you couldn't have done it on your own.'

Why hadn't I asked him before? Fear had stopped me; fear had grown out of all proportion.

Prisoners need releasing or pardoning. They are in a dark place of their own making. The good news is that there is a way out.

EXERCISES

Read Psalm 34 – read it a couple of times and ask the Holy Spirit to show you any verses in particular he wants to use to bring healing to you. Copy the verses out and put them in a place you will see during the week. Use the verses as a prayer in relation to your guilt and pain. Use the verses to receive healing and freedom.

> If we confess our sins, he is faithful and just and will forgive us our sins and purify us from all unrighteousness. (1 John 1:9)

> But with you there is forgiveness. (Psalm 130:4)

> There is now no condemnation for those who are in Christ Jesus. (Romans 8:1)

Here are some questions to ask yourself:

- What are the things in your life that make you feel guilty?
- Can you identify a pattern?
- Do these things remind you of any past feelings?
- In the past, how have you dealt with your feelings of guilt?
- What were your parents'/carers' expectations of you?
- What happened when you said 'sorry' to your parents? Was the relationship restored?
- Was blame and punishment frequent?
- What was the response of Jesus to people who failed?
- What stops you receiving forgiveness and letting go?

Let's pray

Jesus, I come to you and ask that you break now the cycle of guilt and self-blame in my life. I lay down at your feet the opinions of others. (It may help to visualise any family members or people who have blamed you at the cross – you on one side with Jesus, and the family/people on the other side of Jesus. Walk away and leave them with Jesus. If you don't visualise things, just say out loud, 'I am bringing these people to you, Jesus, and leaving them with you, along with their blame and expectations of me.') *I choose to receive your affirmation of love and acceptance. Amen.* (Wait on him as you receive.)

2: Facing Shame

Isaiah 61 speaks of prisoners and captives. We've looked at being a prisoner, but now let's look at being a captive. What is a captive? It is usually someone who is held a prisoner against their will – in this instance they have been sinned against by someone. They haven't done anything wrong, but they are held to ransom.

This can happen via any form of abuse: sexual abuse (rape, molestation or incest), physical abuse (being hit), emotional abuse (a dominant parent or carer who is always angry and controlling, or an alcoholic carer, or a mentally ill carer), or neglect (a carer withholding love and attention).

Real guilt is when we have done something wrong against humankind or God. False guilt, by contrast, is when someone has done something wrong against us, but tells us or makes us feel that we are the guilty one. I have found this to be so common amongst those suffering abuse, many of whom I've ministered to over the years. This means that the abusers absolve themselves of all responsibility. Then they usually go on to abuse someone else.

Why do we believe them when they tell us that it was entirely our fault? Maybe because when we're children, we look up to adults. We believe them. We think that they will tell us the truth.

These are some of the things that I have heard abused people say:

- 'I must have been really bad for my dad to keep having to beat me up. I probably deserved it. He said I would never learn. It must have been true. He said if I told my mum she would leave him and me and it would be all my fault.'

- 'It must have been all my fault that my uncle sexually abused me, because he said I was very flirtatious when I was seven years old. He said that I wanted him to hug and touch me. He said it was his way of showing me that he loved me. He said that I must not tell anyone, or else people would know that I made him do it.'

- 'My dad said it was our little secret. It was how daddies showed their children how they loved them. If I told anyone our little secret, they wouldn't understand and something bad would happen to me.'

- 'I knew when I was sent to the neighbours by my mum to get something that I would be taken into the garden shed and abused. Why did I go? Why didn't I say "no"? Why didn't I tell my mum? It must have been my fault.'

- 'I must be really stupid. Those girls/boys used to like me. I must be like they say I am. I must have done something wrong, as they used to be my friends. Now they just call me bad names like "whore" or "bitch". Sometimes they kick me in class. They say if I tell, something worse will happen to me.'

The problem is, we believe the lies we are fed by our abusers. We expected adults or our friends to tell us the truth. We expected our carers to rescue us or to guess what was wrong.

Abusers lie to us. When we are continually lied to, it becomes a belief – a wrong belief, and out of our wrong beliefs we make decisions.

For example, when we are growing up adults tell us, 'Don't touch the cooker when it's on – it will burn you.' We believe them, and we don't touch the cooker. Is this a wrong belief? No, it is not. But what about 'Don't tread on cracks in the pavement – it will make you go blind'? Did your friends or family tell you that one? I've seen people who still avoid cracks in the pavement when they're over 30 years old! We can very easily grow up believing things that are actually not true.

In South Africa I met a very distressed young Zulu girl whose mother had died. Her sister consistently accused her of causing her mother's death. When I asked what her mother had died from, she said it had been 'alcohol poisoning of the liver'. At the time of her mother's death, her sister was out at a friend's house. Her sister was always out and made her sibling stay at home with their sick mother.

I asked the girl, 'When did your mum start to be an alcoholic?'

She replied, 'It was before she got married and had children.'

Shocked that she could think she was to blame, I said to her, 'How could it possibly be your fault? Your mother was responsible for her own health. She chose to abuse her body with alcohol long before you were born.'

She sobbed and sobbed. It took a while of prayer for her to relinquish that responsibility – to give to Jesus what she had taken upon herself. She had taken it upon herself to be responsible just because her sister had said so, but Jesus set her free of that false guilt. It seemed obvious to me that her sister also felt guilty because she had been out at a friend's house during her mother's illness, and she had passed this guilt on to her younger sister so that she could remain free.

Have you done that? Have you taken responsibility that was not yours to take?

Let's pray

Jesus, please bring to mind now anyone for whom I have taken responsibility. (Take time to let the Holy Spirit show you anyone whom you carry as a burden – someone's well-being, or someone whose death you feel responsible for.) *I bring them to you now, Jesus, at the cross. I choose to let go of them now.* (Out loud declare their name and say, 'I am not responsible for N. I hand him/her over to you now, Jesus.')

Receive that release and liberty. We are not meant to carry people about with us, as it causes us to be what the Bible describes as 'weak and heavy laden'. Carrying burdens of false guilt wears us out.

Another person who carried false guilt around with him was Andy. He had suffered from a severe compulsive disorder for about ten years, for which he had to take medication. This disorder interfered with his everyday life and he really wanted to be free from it. After a while of praying, I had a sense from the Holy Spirit that Andy had suffered grief as a young child. He explained that his mother had had an affair with a married pastor of a church. Before Andy was born, this cowardly pastor ran away from both his wife and Andy's mum, never to be seen again. As he told me this story, another story from the Bible flooded my mind. It concerns the man who was born blind. In the story the man was accused of being 'steeped in sin at his birth'. I realised that this was how Andy thought about himself – he believed that he was the result of sin. He carried a massive amount of false guilt and shame. This had become his identity. Initially Andy had to give up this as his identity, so that he could find out who he really was. It was a struggle for him, as this was all he had ever known. If he gave it up, who would he be?

Later on, in the chapter about absent parents, I will continue Andy's story, and in the last chapter we will look at our identity.

Another guy I met was Peter. He was neglected by both parents when he was a child. He was left one evening, at the age of five, to babysit for his younger brother and his sister, who was only two years old. Imagine his fear when his baby sister started crying in her cot and he didn't know where his parents were. After a while, he wandered down the street knocking on doors, asking if his parents were there. Eventually he found them at a party. They

LET THE HEALING BEGIN

swore at him because he had disturbed their fun. This little boy thought he was in the wrong for not being able to help his baby sister. He felt responsible even at the age of five. He was never shown any love or affection. His parents played mind games with him and he was always in the wrong. If I asked him what he thought of this sort of treatment, he would say, 'That's just how it was.' He never blamed them for all the times they neglected him. He had no expectation of life being any different. Later on we will find out how Jesus healed him.

In the Bible Jesus says that if anyone sins against little ones they should have a huge stone tied around their neck and be flung into the sea. That is how angry Jesus is that people abuse children.

If you are remembering things that happened to you as a child and in your head you hear words that say it was all your fault, you need to hear this: *That is a lie.* In Jesus' name, I declare to you now that it is a lie. It wasn't your fault.

What do we do with these lies that assail us in our thought patterns?

In the Bible it says that Jesus is the way, the truth and the life. Jesus not only tells the truth, he is the truth. This is one of the names he calls himself.

In the Bible two of the names given to Satan or the devil are liar and deceiver. It says that Satan is the father of lies: he sires them.

So who are you going to believe, Jesus the truth or Satan the liar? Let's choose to believe Jesus now; let's be free of those lies.

Let's pray

Holy Spirit, please come and show me the lies that I have believed about myself. Jesus, please bring to the surface those lies that are buried deep down in my mind. (As you remember any lies, say out loud, 'In Jesus' name, I renounce the lie of . . .') Jesus, please break the power of that lie now, and release me from it. I surrender the lie that I was to blame. Please forgive me, Jesus, for believing that lie. I receive your forgiveness. Please wash me clean from everything that lie has done to me in my life. Thank you that you are the truth. Fill me with the truth now. Thank you, Lord. I let go of this false guilt, Jesus. Please break it in me. I bring it to the cross – put it to death in me. Thank you, Lord. Amen.

In our thought pattern, if we are having a thought, we refer to ourselves in the first person, as 'I'. If Satan speaks to us in our thought pattern, however, he refers to us as 'you'. During the next few weeks, be aware of the times when Satan is speaking to you. He does it to us all. He is called the accuser of the brethren. This is another of his names. When you have these thought patterns, just say, 'In Jesus' name, I tell you to stop it.'

We are told in the Bible that Satan accuses us day and night – he prowls around like a lion, waiting to devour us. One of the ways he does this is by accusing us and making us feel guilty. Sometimes I hear Christians say, 'I am under attack.' We all are; that is not a new thing.

Let's pray

Jesus, I have listened to the accuser's voice. I am sorry. Please make me aware of my thought patterns this week. Show me when I am agreeing with these accusations. Show me the pattern of accusations that I have been agreeing with. Break that cycle in me, please, Lord. I want to be free of them and say 'no'. Amen.

Being shamed and humiliated

Being shamed goes very deep inside us. It hinders us and stops us looking into the eyes of Jesus, because we don't think we're good enough. Many of us have probably been shamed in some way.

Our daughter Beth was always very quiet at school. She was picked on by a teacher and made to stand up in front of the class. She never put her hand up to ask a question, and the teacher decided that he would try and break this pattern. He said to her, 'You will stand there until you say something.' Underneath the desk, some boys started to kick her ankles. She didn't speak, she just died a death inside. Unknown to us, the teacher continued to humiliate her over the next few days. The other children realised she would make a good victim, so they carried on where the teacher left off. Boys would taunt her with cruel words: 'Your coat is ugly . . . your shoes are ugly . . . your face is ugly.' Girls who were her friends at church suddenly started to follow the lead of a bully. One day they would call Beth over to their group and include her in their activities. The next day they would call her over and then say, 'What are you doing here? We don't want to be with you, go away!' The tall bully would walk behind Beth and kick her legs.

This went on for a few months without us knowing. She always denied that anything was wrong at school, although at home she seemed to be distressed. Beth started to have regular migraine headaches when she was ten. After the six-week summer break, she refused to get out of the car when I took her back to school. Finally the truth came out. Things had become so bad that we had no choice but to take her away from that environment and move her to a smaller local school. She had reached a point when, at just ten years old, she no longer wanted to live. This experience caused years of pain and etched into her a very low self-image.

I had also been humiliated by a teacher at school. When I was asked a question, my mind went blank. To further the humiliation, I was called out to the front of the class and the question was repeated: 'How many pints are in a gallon, Jeannie?' I could barely remember the day of the week, let alone the answer to her question. Fear gripped my stomach as my brain refused to come up with the answer. The teacher then produced two pint milk bottles and told me to go and fetch some water in them until the gallon container was full. I will never forget how many pints are in a gallon, but it took 30 years for that humiliation to rise to the surface and get healed. In fact, the memory returned while I was reading a book by Mary Pytches called *Yesterday's Child*. Tears started to flow down my cheeks. I sobbed out my humiliation and asked Jesus to come and heal me. I remembered the classroom and sensed Jesus there with me. Instead of feeling weak and foolish, I experienced his love for me. I experienced his comfort. Then I forgave that teacher for causing me pain.

Many of us have suffered the pain of our so-called friends rejecting us one day and being friends again the next, or a teacher or a parent humiliating us.

Let's pray
Remember that painful time at school or at home, and ask the Holy Spirit to come and bring that memory to the surface. Ask Jesus to come and visit that memory. Jesus is not ashamed of you.

For some of us, the thought of looking Jesus in the eyes makes us feel ashamed. We think Jesus is ashamed of us. He is not. We have no evidence that he thinks that way.

Jesus was not ashamed of Zacchaeus. He was the guy who had to climb a tree because he was too short to see above the crowd that had gathered to see Jesus. As I thought about Zacchaeus, I had the impression that at school he had been rejected – perhaps he was picked on because of his size. Maybe his stature made him feel inferior to other people. It's interesting that he went on to cheat people out of money when he was older. It's as if he was trying to make himself seem bigger, more important, or superior. We are told that he was a tax collector, so it was probably easy to cheat people. I think he then felt ashamed of what he had done. Being ashamed cut him off from good relationships. It's interesting that he had no friends to lift him up above the crowds. He was alone. Jesus didn't say he was ashamed of him, though. Jesus said, 'I'm coming to your house for tea.' He wanted a relationship with Zacchaeus. Jesus also knew that

FACING SHAME

Zacchaeus lacked friends. He knew that Zacchaeus didn't have people coming round to his house for tea; he knew that he was despised. Jesus could see beyond that shame. The result was that Zacchaeus changed and gave people their money back. In fact, he gave them back even more money than he had taken. The love of Jesus and his mercy changed Zacchaeus into a generous man.

Maybe you were ashamed of a parent, maybe you never asked anyone home to your house for tea. It wasn't until I wrote this that I realised I never used to ask anyone to my house. My mum wasn't like other mums. She didn't go out. She often took to her bed with depression. Such differences can make us feel cut off from other people.

In the Bible we read about the man who was blind from birth. The disciples asked Jesus, 'Did this man sin, or was it his parents?' This man was judged as having committed a sin just because he was born with a physical affliction. He was bullied. This man must have felt like an outcast. He wasn't even allowed inside the Temple – he had to stay outside begging. That's how it feels when you are made to feel like an outcast. Yet Jesus healed that man. He healed his sight so that he could see Jesus. This wasn't just a physical healing. Jesus took away all the false accusations and the lies. Then that man was able to see Jesus.

Let's pray

Jesus, please come with the light of your love now. Come to those places inside me that were emotionally abused or neglected. Shine the light of your love. Show me how acceptable I am to you. Where I feel different from others, start your healing process in me. Amen.

I have met and prayed with many people who were sexually abused. In the Bible, in the Song of Solomon, it says, 'Do not awaken love until it so desires.'

In 2 Samuel 13 we are told the story of Amnon, who fell in love with his half-sister Tamar (although this sounds like a TV soap story, it really is in the Bible). As the story unfolds, you will see it was not love but lust that motivated Amnon.

Amnon's sinful lust for his half-sister made him ill. Tamar was a virgin and this tormented Amnon; he wanted her first, before anyone else. Amnon told his friend how he felt. The friend also sinned and told Amnon to trick Tamar. He said, 'Tell her you feel ill and get your sister to come and feed you.' So he did. Tamar leaned over him with some food and Amnon grabbed her and tried to tempt her into bed with him.

Tamar said, 'Don't force me, don't do this wicked thing. I will be disgraced.' She even gave him a way out: 'Ask the king and he will let you marry me.'

But Amnon refused to listen. He thought with his body instead of his brain. Since he was the strongest, he raped her.

What was the outcome? Did he love her more? No. The Bible says that Amnon hated her with an intense hatred. He said to Tamar, 'Get up and get out.'

Still she tried to save him: 'No,' she said, 'sending me away will be a greater wrong than you have already done me.' She wanted the truth to be known, for him to face the consequences.

Amnon refused to listen. He no longer wanted to look at what he had done. He blamed Tamar, who had done no wrong, for his own sin. He sent her away and locked the door.

Tamar's robe was torn. It was the type of robe that was only worn by virgins and daughters of the king. She ripped it, symbolic of what had happened to her virginity. She had been robbed of that part of her identity, of who she was. No longer could she wear that type of robe. She put ashes on her head (that's what they did in those days when they were mourning a loss). She mourned and wept for what she had lost. She mourned the loss of her virginity and the loss of her relationship with her brother. She must have felt unclean and ashamed. She left weeping loudly.

Her blood-brother Absalom guessed what must have happened to her and said, 'Be quiet now, my sister. He is your brother. Don't take this to heart.'

Don't take this to heart? What? He was saying, 'It doesn't matter. Forget it. It's not that bad.' Absalom's attitude makes me want to shout from the rooftops: 'Yes it is that bad! No she doesn't need to be quiet!'

Tamar was not allowed to grieve or get angry. What was the result of that upon her? It says in the Bible that Tamar lived the rest of her life a desolate woman. The dictionary definition of 'desolate' is 'overwhelmed with grief, neglected, barren, solitary, dreary, dismal, forlorn'.

Tamar needed to let rip with her pain, grief and anger, not hold it in!

Nowadays we know that the best thing for Tamar would have been for her to tell others, to inform the king, to get justice and allow herself to let out her pain.

This story makes me so upset and angry, because I know

that this same thing happens to so many young girls and guys today.

As the verse from the Song of Songs says, 'Do not awaken love until it so desires.' But many of us didn't awaken our bodies to sexual touch and desire – someone else did. To be the unwanted object of another's desire can be so painful.

The sexual part of us – our erogenous zones, our feelings and thoughts – was made by God to be woken in a safe, mature environment, within marriage and the parameters of love. Instead, a lot of people are aroused at a young age, before they are ready.

Many people who have been sexually abused are tormented by the memories of how their body responded to the touch of their abuser. I need to tell you that it was OK that your body responded. It was programmed to respond that way, even though you hated what was happening to you and were repulsed by it. Stop blaming yourself for your reactions.

I have prayed with many people who were so disgusted at themselves and repulsed by how their own bodies responded to touch. Their mind and emotions were probably screaming 'No!', but their body was not resisting.

All some people wanted was to be loved and held. Some wanted an expression of love at any price. Some people spend years hating and loathing their bodies, rejecting what God so lovingly made.

God made our bodies and he made us sexual – for our pleasure, and for each other's pleasure within marriage. It was a gift to us that has been abused.

Sometimes, because of the cycle of wanting but hating

what happened, it can start a pattern of seeking out this sort of so-called 'love'. It can get mixed up in our head and we can get confused and start to look for this in other places. We can become promiscuous, always going too far in our relationships and then regretting it and hating ourselves. We can seek alcohol, drugs or food to stop the pain of what happened.

We have to choose with our minds to stop blaming ourselves for this.

Remember the wrong belief. We were made to believe it was our fault. We have been hitting ourselves with a big stick. We were abused and now we are abusing ourselves.

People are bullied because of the clothes they wear, because they are dyslexic, or for the style of their hair, or for a disability, or maybe because they wear glasses. My daughter said that if she was in a Christian meeting and people were giving testimonies about having been sexually abused or raped, she felt a response inside. Even though she had never been sexually abused, she had been robbed. It was like an emotional rape. This is what any form of abuse does to us.

Many people are first abused in one way, and often get abused again in the same way or in a different way. It's as if they have written on their forehead, 'Abuse me.' Others make sure that they will never be hurt again, by becoming like stone emotionally; like a hard rock inside that no one will ever penetrate. They cannot have meaningful relationships. Guys particularly choose to cope in this way.

Jesus showed mercy to people whom others turned away. Faced with promiscuous or abused people, he showed mercy and drew them to himself.

In Mark 5:25 we are told of a woman who must have felt very ashamed. She had been bleeding for twelve years. If you are a woman reading this, can you imagine having a nonstop period for twelve years? For a start, she must have been anaemic and physically drained. She had consulted many doctors, we are told, and she had suffered greatly under their care. She had become worse over the years. I believe she must have experienced an enormous amount of suffering, because in those days issues of blood were thought to be unclean. She must have felt like an outcast. She was following Jesus amongst the crowd. Can you imagine what her life must have been like? Maybe she couldn't get married because of her condition. Maybe she was married and the bleeding started after she had children. It must have affected her sex life. She must have smelt very bad in that heat. Maybe she had been sexually abused and it started after that. Whatever happened, she was feeling desperate. So desperate that she dared to reach out and touch Jesus' robe. In her uncleanness, she reached out and recognised his purity.

When we feel ashamed, this is what we need to do. We need to touch Jesus, who is pure, with our feelings of uncleanliness. If you were made to feel powerless because you were hit, reach out and touch Jesus. If you were over-powered with another's lust and desire, reach out and touch Jesus. If a cruel mind played games with your mind, reach out and touch Jesus.

This suffering woman reached out of her shame for just a moment to touch him, believing that he could heal her. *Immediately* her bleeding stopped and she felt in her body that she was free from her suffering. Two things happened here: the bleeding stopped and she received physical healing, but she was also set free from her suffering, her shame and her disgust.

Jesus looked around. 'Who touched me?' he said. Of course he knew who had touched him. He just wanted her to acknowledge him. When we want to receive healing from Jesus, we need to do that. Doubt is OK, but unbelief is different. We need to say to him, 'Jesus, I am reaching out to you because you can heal me.'

Do you know what Jesus did next? He affirmed her. Jesus always heals what needs healing, not just the things that we think need healing. He said to her, 'Daughter, daughter.' Jesus and the Father are one, so he is ministering the Father's love to her. From this we can see that she needed healing in her identity. Maybe she didn't have a father. Maybe she had a father, but he had never affirmed her or made her feel as if she belonged. Or maybe her father had abused her. We don't know. But we do know that Jesus affirming her was part of the healing process for her. He completed her healing by saying, 'Go in peace and be free of your suffering.' He spoke words of freedom to her to break the power of her suffering.

How can Jesus wash away our shame? He can because he too knew what it was like to be abused. He who knew no shame took our shame upon himself. They tried to shame him on the cross, he was stripped bare, beaten and insulted. He was mocked, lied to, betrayed and suffered a most horrible death. Even now he is still mocked and lies are told about him. He took that shame so that we – you and I – don't have to carry it. Take off now those filthy garments of shame. He offers you clean clothes. Come to the cross with that humiliation and that embarrassment. Look into Jesus' eyes of love. Let his love enfold you.

Let's pray

Jesus, I acknowledge you as my healer. I am reaching out to touch your garment now – to touch you. I confess my unbelief. Please forgive me. You scorned shame on the cross. Jesus, please take my shame now upon yourself. Take my filthy clothes: I choose to take them off and give them to you. Jesus, you are pure – give me clean clothes of purity.

(Take a step towards Jesus. You are acceptable to him; he will not turn you away or reject you; he knows what it is like to be rejected. Receive his affirmation – my son, my daughter. Receive his healing – son of the King, daughter of the King.)

Jesus, please affirm me where I have been frightened or ashamed, the places where I have been bleeding for years. Come with your purity, Jesus. Where I feel unclean and dirty, please cleanse me. I dedicate my abused body to you. I dedicate my mind to you. Jesus, please give me a sound mind. I lift my eyes to you. Cleanse my eyes from all that I have seen that was unhelpful or unclean. Draw from me all the humiliation and take it into yourself, Lord. Amen.

EXERCISES

1. If you have been abusing yourself in any way (e.g. using alcohol, sex, food or drugs, or cutting yourself), confess it now to Jesus. Ask and receive his forgiveness.
2. If you have never told anyone about being abused, then pray and seek the right person to tell – either a

mature person at church, or a secular counsellor. You can always receive prayer alongside secular counselling. Use the Internet or look at lists in your local library. Doctors nowadays can refer you to a counsellor too.

3. Choose to lay down the blame at Jesus' feet.
4. Use some symbols to help as you pray, like bread and wine, or candles and a cross.
5. Some people find it helpful to paint a symbolic picture of their pain, distress or shame. Others find writing helpful. Some people also find it helpful to set fire to what they have drawn or written.
6. We need to get the poison out into the open rather than let it fester and damage us. A good book to read about sexual abuse is *The Wounded Heart*, written by a Christian, Dr Dan B. Allender (published by NavPress). There is also a very good companion workbook called *The Wounded Heart – Hope for Adult Victims of Childhood Sexual Abuse*.

SCRIPTURES

In all their distress he too was distressed,
  and the angel of his presence saved them.
In his love and mercy he redeemed them;
  he lifted them up and carried them
  all the days of old. (Isaiah 63:9)

The LORD is my rock, my fortress and my deliverer;
  my God is my rock, in whom I take refuge. . .
He rescued me from my powerful enemy,
  from my foes who were too strong for me.
They confronted me in the day of my disaster,
  but the LORD was my support. (Psalm 18:2, 17–18)

Trust in him at all times, O people;
   pour out your hearts to him,
   for God is our refuge. (Psalm 62:8)

Then he showed me Joshua . . . standing before the angel of
the LORD, and Satan standing at his right side to accuse him.
The LORD said to Satan, 'The LORD rebuke you, Satan! . . . Is not
this man a burning stick snatched from the fire?'
   Now Joshua was dressed in filthy clothes as he stood before
the angel. The angel said to those who were standing before
him, 'Take off his filthy clothes.'
   Then he said to Joshua, 'See, I have taken away your sin,
and I will put rich garments on you.' (Zechariah 3:1–4)

Let us fix our eyes on Jesus, the author and perfector of our
faith, who for the joy set before him endured the cross, scorn-
ing its shame, and sat down at the right hand of the throne of
God. Consider him who endured such opposition from sinful
men, so that you will not grow weary and lose heart.
(Hebrews 12:2–3)

. . .because God has said,
   'Never will I leave you;
   never will I forsake you.'
So we say with confidence,
   'The Lord is my helper; I will not be afraid.
   What can man do to me?' (Hebrews 13:5–6)

The LORD will not leave the guilty unpunished. (Nahum 1:3)

3: Looking at Our Anger

We need to get into the habit of seeking healing *often* and get out of the habit of waiting to be in a church service. Secular counselling can also be very helpful and we can receive prayer alongside this. We need to identify where our coping strategies are and which areas need healing, and concentrate on one area at a time. We need to make this area our daily prayer until we see that one thing free and healed. It's a good time to bring our healing needs when we take communion at church. The Bible says that 'by his wounds we are healed' (Isaiah 53:5). Communion is a great place to acknowledge what Jesus has done for us in his brokenness and to bring our own brokenness for healing. I personally found this to be a great place for receiving healing.

Of course, it's also good to receive prayer from another Christian, who can be with you as you face any pain from the past. Sometimes, though, we can get into the habit of never bringing our pain to Jesus when we are on our own.

Jesus wants a 'personal' relationship with us. Part of such a personal relationship is receiving that freedom directly from him. He is quite capable of healing us on his own, without needing any assistance!

Some of us get worried that we may scream out, or cry loudly in public when Jesus is healing past hurts. We can be afraid that we may have an evil spirit. Yes, that does happen sometimes, but usually it's old pain being let out that wasn't expressed at the time it happened. Imagine if you shut your finger in a drawer and instead of yelling out the pain, you imploded. That wouldn't be good, would it? Shouting out our pain is a great release. It's OK and good to express our pain from the past.

At St Andrew's Church, where I received a lot of healing, people screamed out their pain or cried when they were getting free; it seemed so normal to do that there. Usually, when we hear people crying in church services or at Christian gatherings, we can have a few different reactions: we may feel embarrassed or scared and want to get away, or we may feel glad it's not happening to us, or we may think, 'Thank goodness I can be real with my pain now.'

Let's be compassionate, and let's be pleased and say 'thank you, Jesus' when we hear others letting out their pain. Let's pray now and say to Jesus that we don't care what it takes, we just want to be free.

Let's pray

Jesus, I admit I'm scared of my feelings. I get frightened that this pain inside me might overwhelm me. I want to be healed, no matter what it takes. I give you permission to release these feelings inside me. Amen.

Sometimes we become scared that we have an evil spirit. We don't need to be afraid of demonic activity.

Sometimes we can act as if Satan and demons are the equal opposite of God. They are not. God is almighty – there is no opposite to him; there is no equal opposite like in *Superman*, where good just about overcomes evil. God is not just good, he is *holy*. Satan is the opposite of a true angel. In fact, he is a fallen angel. He wanted the other angels to worship him instead of all worshipping God. He was then cast out of heaven down to earth (see Isaiah 14:12–14).

The devil, our enemy, Satan, or whatever else you call him, takes advantage of our unconfessed sin. 'Your enemy the devil prowls around like a roaring lion looking for someone to devour' is one of the descriptions of his strategies given in the Bible (see 1 Peter 5:8).

If we have unresolved issues of hatred, anger and bitterness, then we will suffer the consequences of these sins. By leaving them unresolved, we can give the devil a foothold into our lives. In my experience, when someone confesses and repents of sin, then receives forgiveness, their pain is released and anything contrary to the Holy Spirit drops off. It's as if we become too slippery for anything contrary to the Holy Spirit to hang onto. I usually think of such things as 'cling-ons'. Sometimes, though, our pain is released *first*, and *only then* do we feel released to confess our sin and so on.

However, if we have been involved in occult practices or witchcraft, or if our anger is so out of control that we want to kill someone or harm ourselves, then we obviously need to go and see our minister or pastor so that we can receive prayer and deliverance. In the Bible we see Jesus delivering demonised people. We have no need to fear: Jesus is the ultimate, the supreme power. He does it with the power of his love.

I was told recently that Smith Wigglesworth (a well-known Christian whom God used powerfully many years ago) once felt a presence in the bed with him, turned round and said, 'Oh, it's you, Satan,' and turned back over and went to sleep! He had no fear; he knew that he who was inside him was greater than he who was in the world.

The devil can work in the following ways:

- he wants us to ignore him and think he doesn't exist
- he wants us to be frightened of him
- he wants us to be fascinated by him and seek him out

As and when appropriate, we will be talking about the strategies that the enemy uses and how we can be free from demonic influences.

I want now to explore the area of anger and hatred. Christians sometimes have a problem with expressing anger. Some people think it's not good to be angry, because we're Christians. Or else they think that being angry is a sin.

This is not biblical. The Bible says, rather, 'In your anger, do not sin: Do not let the sun go down while you are still angry' (Ephesians 4:26).

Anger is not a sin, but if we hold onto it, then it gives an opportunity for bitterness and hatred to grow. The verse is saying, 'Get rid of it before the day is out. Don't let Satan seize the advantage.'

Maybe you think you don't have a problem with anger.

If I mention driving, motorways, traffic jams, people who don't indicate, elderly drivers and lorry drivers or white-van man, how are you feeling now? Road rage is on the increase. Maybe this is an area you can relate to! Do you fancy rating your aggression level with this little test? Have a look, be honest, and tick how many of these statements apply to you.

Aggressive driving

Which of the following apply to you?[1]

1. Mentally being abusive to other drivers.
2. Verbally demeaning other drivers to your passenger.
3. Denying someone entry into your lane because you are frustrated or annoyed.
4. Giving someone the 'if looks could kill' signal to show your disapproval.
5. Speeding past another car or revving the engine to show your disapproval.
6. Preventing another driver from passing you.
7. Going too close to the car in front to 'persuade' them to go faster.
8. Fantasising violence against another driver.
9. Honking the horn or yelling at another driver.
10. Making a visible gesture with your fingers.
11. Using your car to retaliate by making sudden movements.
12. Pursuing another car in a chase.
13. Getting out of the car for a verbal argument.

---

[1] Adapted from *Anger Workshop Booklet* by Graham Bretherick, used by permission.

LET THE HEALING BEGIN

14. Carrying a weapon 'just in case you need it'.
15. Deliberately bumping another car in anger.
16. Trying to run another car off the road.
17. Getting out of the car and hitting someone.
18. Trying to run someone down.
19. Shooting at a car.
20. Killing someone.

How did you do? We may look at the last six or seven points and think that we would never do such a thing. But look at the stages that lead up to those violent actions. In a test that was done outside the UK, the majority of drivers got as far as step 13.

We all get angry, but is it God-given? Do you know what happens to our bodies when we get angry? Anger is energy in our body that protects us from danger. It's also a way of giving us a safety valve.

In 1 Samuel 11:6 we see that Saul saw his people frightened and threatened and about to follow someone else. The power of God came upon Saul and he 'burned with anger'. This gave him energy to act, and he took a pair of oxen and cut them into pieces.

Did you notice that it was not a little rabbit he chopped up, but *two oxen*. They were huge for one man to cut up, but the power of God and the energy of the anger gave Saul the strength he needed. He cut the oxen into little pieces and had them distributed via messengers. It was a very strong message: 'If you don't follow me into battle, then this is what will be done to your oxen.' The oxen were the people's livelihood. Needless to say, they obeyed the message!

Anger is a form of stress reaction. When we get angry, a lot of different things happen in our body:

- Adrenalin epinephrine is pumped into the body. It increases the heart rate, enlarges pupils and increases mental accuracy.
- Cortisol is given out into the body, activating the immune system and increasing blood flow.
- Glucagon is released into the body, releasing sugar (energy) from the liver into the bloodstream.
- Thyroxin is freed into the body. It regulates our metabolism to keep things in balance during the stress period.
- The pituitary gland is activated, releasing hormones that trigger the other hormones to energise us.

Wow! That's amazing, isn't it?

Our confusion with anger comes when we misunderstand what anger is and fail to understand how it should be expressed. Anger expressed wrongly brings destruction.

Saul spoke to his son Jonathan about David. Instead of reading the following passage in a polite, quiet voice in your head, try shouting it out angrily. Then you will get more of an idea of how this must have sounded.

Saul's anger flared up [it was already there if it 'flared up'] at Jonathan and he said to him, 'You son of a perverse and rebellious woman! Don't I know that you have sided with the son of Jesse to your own shame and to the shame of the mother who bore you? As long as the son of Jesse [David] lives on this earth, neither you nor your kingdom will be established. Now send and bring him to me, for he must die!'

'Why should he be put to death? What has he done?'

Jonathan asked his father. But Saul hurled his spear at him to kill him. Then Jonathan knew that his father intended to kill David. (1 Samuel 20:30–33)

Surely that last sentence must be the understatement of the year!

And Saul tried to kill David more than once. I would suggest that this was the wrong way to express anger. When it is used as God intended, however, anger can energise us for good.

In 1 Samuel 20:34, we are told that Jonathan got up from the table 'in fierce anger'. He had a right to be angry – his father had not only just tried to kill him, but was also intent on killing his best friend. What did Jonathan do with his anger? The Bible tells us that on the second day of the month Jonathan didn't eat. He didn't need to, as he had energy from the anger. The passage then says that he took time to grieve: he let out, in private, his feelings of anger and pain. He didn't direct them onto anyone else. Notice that he let the anger out. He didn't just swallow it and allow it to fester.

I can't remember many times when I have let my anger out in a good way, but someone reminded me recently of a time when I did. With a friend, we had organised the first New Wine conference. We had no experience of doing such a thing before, and our resources were low. Every day was a new experience in administration. When we started, I didn't even know how to work a computer, let alone order equipment and organise an exhibition. When the time came for the conference to start, I felt completely drained.

Unfortunately, I happened to be in the information

office on the first day when the delegates were arriving. In hindsight, it was the worst place for me to be, as I felt I had already given my all and took even the slightest complaint too personally. In came a group of Norwegians. Putting a big smile on my face, I asked if I could be of help. 'Yes please,' one of the young men said. 'Where have you put our tents? We have been looking for them, but we can't find them.'

Still with a smile, I replied, 'What village are you in?'

He replied quickly, 'We're not in a village, we have just arrived from the airport.'

Slowly it was dawning on me. These Norwegians had arrived with no camping equipment; they were expecting us to provide them with everything – tents, sleeping bags, the lot!

I burst out, 'Excuse me a moment!' and walked behind the screen and out of another door. 'AAAARRRRGGGGH-HHH!' I screamed at the top of my voice. Then I returned to the office now full of Norwegians. 'I'm so sorry,' I said. 'We haven't actually got any tents for you. Please excuse me. Pauline here will help you now.' Then I ran from there as fast as I could. I was not proud of myself, but I realised that if I had stayed, I would have said something I would have regretted.

Can you imagine what would have happened if I hadn't let that anger and frustration out and had just swallowed it instead? That anger was an explosion and it could have done me, and those around me, some damage!

I realised a few years ago that I didn't actually display anger many times when it would have been appropriate. What I usually did was to feel really upset and want to cry or run away. The appropriate emotion or feeling should have been anger, but that wasn't available to me. It was as if I felt I deserved what was being dished out to me, or else my head would feel as if it would burst and I would want to run away. Because I didn't express the emotion of anger, it affected my feelings of worth. If we don't express our anger, we can internalise it and bury it. This can then cause a self-loathing instead of a self-liking and affect our sense of worth. There is a whole chapter on self-worth further on in this book.

What if someone sinned against us in our childhood and we have this huge explosion of anger that wants to let rip, but we swallow it instead? What if another bad thing, and then another bad thing, happens? Where does the anger go if we don't let it out?

Psychologists say that *every violation of our person automatically releases anger in us.*

Anger can be expressed in different ways. *Rage* is an active anger and can be very frightening to observe (we have seen what happens in road rage). It can also result in sexual or physical abuse, swearing, yelling, and threatening behaviour or vandalism.

At this point we may be pleased with ourselves if we don't indulge in any of the above, but what about this next expression of anger? It's called being *passive aggressive*. This is an indirect form of anger. It can show itself in sarcasm, procrastinating (putting off and delaying), gossiping, spending money excessively, or maybe shoplifting, making others look stupid or helpless, or having affairs when married.

In 1 Kings 21:1–4 we are shown someone sulking, sullen

and angry and refusing to eat because he was rejected. We can see here that rejection from others can make us angry, and then we *take that anger out on ourselves*.

I was at a conference a couple of years ago and prayed with a youth leader called Becki. Her mother was dying of cancer and was in hospital. Becki so wanted to talk with her mother, to tell her about her life and share with her all the things she'd never told her before. The problem was that although she wanted to, she couldn't. It really worried her, as she didn't know what the barrier was. I asked her about her past. This is her story. When she was a young girl, she was waiting at the tennis court for her mother to pick her up. She didn't come, and Becki waited for two hours, feeling more and more desperate. Eventually, her mother arrived and explained that her father had been rushed to hospital with a heart attack and he died an hour later. Two weeks later, Becki was at the train station waiting for her mother to pick her up. This time Becki waited an hour, feeling more and more desperate and angry. When her mother eventually arrived, she explained to Becki that she had mistakenly gone to the bus station and apologised for being late.

I asked Becki what she had done with all that anger and pain. She said, 'As I got into the car, I decided I would never share anything with my mother again.' And she didn't. Even 30 years later, she was still punishing her mother for letting her dad die; for leaving her frightened and alone. Now she wanted to share everything with her mother, but she couldn't.

I asked her about her anger. Who was she angry with? She started to cry as she admitted she was angry with her father for leaving her and dying, angry with her mother, and even angry with herself.

Becki then asked Jesus to forgive her for her anger. Then she forgave her mother and father for letting her down and causing her to suffer. She let out her pain and forgave herself. Afterwards, she said she felt as if an enormous burden had been lifted from her. She was now ready to share her life with her mother.

Another way of expressing of anger is *to abuse ourselves in our minds*. We can give ourselves personal put-downs, low self-esteem, and make ourselves feel a failure, by listening over and over to past criticism in our head as if it's a negative tape recording. Sometimes we can keep failing at something we are capable of: punishing ourselves. This can lead to feelings of helplessness and even to thoughts of suicide.

In the Bible we see Cain in Genesis 4 as an angry person whose face is 'downcast'. He allows his mind to dwell on his anger and it changes his personality. Even after God shows him a way out, he persists and allows sin to take hold of him. Read the account to find out where his anger leads him.

Another example from the Bible is Jonah. He was so angry, he wanted to die. Look at the story in Jonah 4:1–11 and note the way God speaks to Jonah and questions him.

God asks him, 'Have you any right to be angry?' If we have been sinned against, then yes we have. We need to express that anger. Express it to God, or to someone else. In Jonah's case, however, he had no right to be angry.

Sometimes, we spend our time as an adult trying to justify why we shouldn't be angry, when the fact is that deep inside us we have a fierce or simmering anger that is being denied. At least Jonah was letting his anger out and expressing it. Initially, though, he ran away. He didn't want to admit that he was angry.

At another Soul Survivor conference, a girl was obviously manifesting demonic activity. It didn't take a lot of discernment. As I approached her and looked at her, although she was quite tiny she took a swing at me, but fortunately missed hitting me full on in the face. It took three of us to get her to a place where she wasn't in full view of everyone. We didn't want her to become a spectacle and were anxious to protect her dignity. There were about three different demons that I commanded to leave, and she fell to the ground in a relaxed heap. We then prayed for Jesus to heal her of whatever had caused this in the first place. When she recovered, she told us that she had been sexually abused the year before. Later on, I discovered that this girl had attempted to take her own life earlier on in the day, but had felt a supernatural force restraining her – like a hand on her forehead.

The following year, at the same conference, I came across this same girl during the ministry time. Again she was displaying demonic manifestations. I met up with her to talk about what was going on. Katie told me that she had been abused again, sexually. We talked about her anger. Recently she had felt so angry that she had smashed her hand through a huge mirror. This had caused damage to her hand. Her anger was now being expressed through self-abuse.

After further talking, I discovered that she had been abused as a child. For some reason, she had buried the memories of this time, probably because it was too painful. I asked her what she had done with her anger when she was young. She said that she would get inside a wardrobe in her bedroom. This made her feel safe. Katie had felt powerless when she had been abused, and the anger made her feel powerful. She liked it. After the first time of being delivered of the demons, she had once more felt powerless and had no one to help her with her negative feelings of self-worth. When she was abused again, she allowed that anger to dominate her: once again she had a power she could use.

Katie repented of her anger and confessed her use of it in a wrong way to punish herself and others around her. She chose to visit that place of her childhood, to go to the wardrobe and tell that little girl who was so frightened that she could come out of the wardrobe now. Katie forgave herself as that abused little girl. She forgave the weakness, and saw that she had rejected that part of herself which she had despised. After the ministry time, I talked with some people who were going to help her with her self-worth and self-image issues. It was obviously going to take a while to repair the damage, but she had made a big start.

Our anger can affect our body by causing illnesses. This is not to say that in every case this is the source of the illness, but it may be a contributary factor. Doctors say that anger can trigger headaches, migraines, ulcers, colitis, high blood pressure, cancer, anorexia, bulimia, overeating, backache, and neck or jaw problems.

An example of this is the story of Uzziah, told in 2 Chronicles 26:19–21. Uzziah was unfaithful and proud; he went into the Temple and up to the altar. He was confronted by 80 priests who were trying to stop him performing a ceremony that only the consecrated priests were allowed to do. Uzziah became angry and went into a rage against the priests. Leprosy broke out on his forehead. He had to live in isolation, and had the leprosy until the day he died.

So far, it all sounds rather scary, doesn't it? The point of all this is to identify whether we have anger inside us. Maybe we have denied that we have it from past hurts. Maybe we have expressed this anger as something else, because that something else is more acceptable to us.

I remember a family who were a very lovely Christian family, if a little bit sweet and sugary at times. During a prayer ministry time, I realised that the mother, Lindy, had suffered from having wrong expectations forced upon her as a child. Although on the outside Lindy projected a sugary sweetness, on the inside she was a very angry person. Lindy was a perfectionist, towards herself and her family. The person with whom Lindy was angry was her mother, but she was in complete denial about it. Lindy was a Christian; in her mind Christians didn't do things like that. For her it wasn't the right Christian response.

After a while of praying, I asked Lindy to imagine her mother as something else – maybe an animal, or anything else in creation. She started to laugh in a satisfied way. She imagined her mother as a performing sea lion and saw herself as the trainer. Lindy had a wonderful time putting the sea lion (her mother) through its paces. Then, instead of laughing, Lindy suddenly changed and started to get angry with her mother and started telling her that she wasn't going to continue living up to her expectations. She was going to make her own choices about her life. She told her mother that she had no right to try and control her and she wasn't going to let her do it any more. After the ministry time, Lindy felt that she could now make her own choices.

If we learn a bit about anger, we can then identify it and find out why we are angry. Has stuff happened in the past that causes us to act the way we do now?

Stop and ask Jesus now.

Let's pray
Please come, Holy Spirit. Jesus, please show me anything that happened in the past that is still causing me to be angry now. Show me any areas that I have denied. What am I angry about? I ask you to show me any patterns of anger during the week ahead. Show me which things I need to repent of and which things need releasing. Amen.

We don't need to strive, or go digging about in our past, looking for anger. We can allow the Holy Spirit to show us. Also we don't have to have healing for every single thing that has happened to us, just the key times.

Do we have a pattern of expressing anger that needs to be dealt with? Anger gets us ready to act. It prepares us to deal with danger. There are three types of danger:

- real danger – our life is in danger of being snuffed out
- potential danger – something could be dangerous
- perceived danger – it isn't really dangerous, we just think it might be

Our anger empowers us to act against the danger, because our fear often holds us back. In Nehemiah 5:1–8, we see that Nehemiah became angry at the injustice he saw and it empowered him to act – he used the power of the anger to give him enough energy and courage to sort things out. What we do with this power of anger is a choice we make. Maybe in the past we made a wrong choice concerning what we did with our anger. When our anger is buried, we can end up using it in unconscious ways. If we felt insecure or out of control, we might have used our anger to control. In Proverbs 29:11 we are told that anger is not to control us: we are to control the anger.

Burying our anger is the worst way to deal with it. We may believe that our anger is negative and destructive, or we are afraid of it. Maybe we just don't understand it. Our anger is dangerous when we deny it, suppress it or bury it. Even if we put it out of our mind, it can still operate in us unconsciously.

Imagine a barrel full of anger from past hurts. Every day, we may lift up the lid and ladle off a little of our held-in anger, but that will not get rid of it. What we need is a tap at the bottom of the barrel so that we can let it out – all of it.

Anger is normal. How we express our anger is something we learn at home as we are growing up. How our family expresses anger is something we observe and copy. What model have we learned? Is it safe to express it?

EXERCISES
Look at the worksheet below and write the answers on a separate sheet, either by yourself, or get a couple of your

friends to join in and do it too, so that you can discuss it together.

ANGER WORKSHEET

How was anger expressed in your family?

1. Expression of anger not acceptable or allowed in our house.
2. Expression of anger was only allowed by the adults.
3. Anger expression usually involved shouting.
4. Anger expression was seen in our family as a sign of weakness.
5. We were made to feel ashamed when we expressed anger.
6. Anger expression often involved violence, throwing things.
7. Anger usually resulted in receiving a lecture.
8. Anger was often expressed by someone going into a depression.
9. Anger was expressed by someone withdrawing.
10. People were usually ill after expressing anger.

My father expressed his anger in the following ways:

My mother expressed her anger in the following ways:

When I was a child I expressed my anger in the following ways:

My parents responded to my anger by:

As an adult I believe anger is: (e.g. bad to express, makes me feel guilty, makes things worse, should be avoided)

Your family's view of anger will affect your current view of anger. For example, if your parents expressed their anger through rage, you may do the same thing, or you may try to avoid rage expression at all costs.

My parents expressed anger by:

So now I express anger by:

Now when someone gets angry with me I usually:

Replay the last week in your mind and see if you can recall at least five things that made your 'anger' button go off.

Is it hard for you to recall when your 'anger' button goes off?

What do you think might happen to you if you allowed yourself to acknowledge that you are angry more often than you do now?[2]

---

[2] Some of the exercises given above have been adapted from the anger management workshop by Graham Bretherick which I attended in summer 2001. Graham is a chartered psychologist and has been a speaker at New Wine, Canada.

LET THE HEALING BEGIN

4: **Allowing Inner Healing**

What is 'inner healing'? I believe it is a process in which the Holy Spirit brings forgiveness of sins and emotional healing to people who have suffered damage to their mind, spirit and soul. It can include a whole range of things, including deliverance, release from bondages and freedom from vows made in the past. It can also include the breaking of strong emotional ties. In some cases, it involves healing of certain memories and releasing stored-up anger. The results are life changing, as the restraints of pain from the past no longer affect the present. It enables us to make better choices and break free from harmful patterns of behaviour.

We need to know that inner healing is a process: it doesn't happen all at once. We are made body, spirit and soul, and when bad things happen to us the whole of us is affected. What we need is wholeness in every area that has been affected. We all have the potential for wholeness, although we will not be completely whole until we get to heaven.

What are the differences between our body, spirit and soul?

- Body: our body enables us to have an awareness of the world around us through all of our senses: hearing, seeing, smelling, tasting and touching.
- Spirit: our spirit (which also includes our conscience) enables us to have an awareness of God and to have interaction with him.
- Soul: our soul enables us to have self-awareness through our mind, emotions and will.

In 1 Thessalonians 5:23 we read, 'May God himself, the God of peace, sanctify you through and through. May your whole spirit, soul and body be kept blameless at the coming of our Lord Jesus Christ.'

For some of us an analogy of inner healing is this: When we became a Christian, we invited Jesus into our body. Our body is a temple for the Holy Spirit to dwell in; another word for 'temple' could be 'house'. We may have invited Jesus to come and live in our 'house', our body, but how many other rooms have we allowed him to come into? Have we allowed him into our soul, our innermost being? Our soul, as we just learned, is our mind, our emotions and our will.

Let's just pray now and invite Jesus into some more rooms.

Let's pray
Holy Spirit, thank you that you live in me. Jesus, I give you permission now to go into more rooms – rooms that are shut off inside me, my mind, emotions and will. I need your transforming power, your healing touch and presence. I open myself up to you now – I open up my memories for you to heal. I want more of you in my life, past and present. Amen.

Some of you reading this may have sought the spirit world before you became a Christian. You may have been involved with occult-linked practices in the past that you have never confessed to Jesus. Maybe you relied on horoscopes, attended a séance, had your palm read or consulted the spirit world involving tarot card reading or a Ouija board. Perhaps you practised some Eastern therapy. Others may have been involved in a cult or sect – perhaps Jehovah's Witnesses or Mormons. In other words, you may have sought power or comfort from a place other than God. You may have worshipped what the Bible calls 'idols' or 'other gods'. An idol can be something to which we give a lot of our time, devotion and energy, something that we honour above anything else. Take a couple of minutes and ask the Holy Spirit to show you anything that you have made a 'god' or 'idol' in your life.

> When men tell you to consult mediums and spiritists, who whisper and mutter, should not a people enquire of their God? Why consult the dead on behalf of the living? To the law and to the testimony! If they do not speak according to this word, they have no light of dawn. Distressed and hungry, they will roam through the land; when they are famished, they will become enraged and, looking upward, will curse their king and their God. Then they will look towards the earth and see only distress and darkness and fearful gloom, and they will be thrust into utter darkness. (Isaiah 8:19–22)

> You shall have no other gods before me. You shall not make for yourself an idol . . . You shall not bow down to them or worship them; for I, the LORD your God, am a jealous God. (Exodus 20: 3–5)

Deuteronomy 18:10 speaks of divination and sorcery and other practices that are detestable to the Lord.

Divination is seeking revelation by supernatural means other than the Holy Sprit. Sorcery is bringing people under control using a spell. This could be through witch-craft, but could also happen through abusing oneself with drugs or being addicted to hypnotic music, and so on.

If any of this applies to you, just say the following prayer.

Let's pray

Dear Father, I come to you now in the name of Jesus and confess that I have sought comfort or experiences through seeking the spirit world. You say in your Word that this is abhorrent to you, you hate and detest it. I am so sorry that I have sought power and supernatural experiences other than the Holy Spirit. Please forgive me. I repent of these practices and I turn away from them. I choose you, Jesus, over all these things. You are the source of life. You are the way, the truth and the life. Break the power of darkness in me, Jesus. Cleanse me by your blood. Thank you that you died on the cross for me. Thank you that you forgive my sin. (If appropriate, renounce in Jesus' name those prac-tices that you have followed, and say that you choose to have nothing more to do with them.) *Fill me now with your Holy Spirit. Thank you, Jesus. Amen.*

Please note: if you have been involved in any of the above-mentioned practices, it would be beneficial for you to speak with your minister or pastor and get him/her to pray with you and for you as you renounce these practices.

If you find it a struggle speaking with your minister, then a really helpful book to read is *Demolishing Strongholds* by David Devenish, which includes a very useful study guide.

If you have any books, videos, icons, jewellery, or anything at all to do with any of these practices, get rid of them by burning them or completely destroying them.

Even when we were newborn babies, we were affected by our time in the womb or by our delivery. Not all of us need healing from it, although I have discovered that some of us do.

Our desire was for unconditional love. Who can give this to us? God definitely can, but because we aren't perfect, humans can't usually give us this sort of love. Everything we received from conception that did not come from unconditional love had the potential to hurt us and scar us.

Research on the subject has discovered that unborn babies can suffer stress while in the womb. If the mother experiences stress and trauma, then chemicals are released through the umbilical cord (the lifeline) to the baby. Recently on television, they showed a baby's facial expressions inside the womb, and even when the mother's stomach was being examined the baby's face showed signs of discomfort.

Some mothers may be victims of abuse, so they are in a state of constant fear and anxiety. Sometimes, because her previous pregnancy or labour experience was traumatic, a mother can be constantly stressed about the child in her womb and what might happen in the future. Maybe the child in the womb was never wanted or planned.

On a few occasions, I have prayed for people about when they were a baby in the womb. Usually the person for whom I'm praying has initiated it. Sometimes people have had sensations of a cord around their neck during the prayer ministry time and sense that they are in a strange place, where they feel they are being squeezed. Others have continuing experiences of waking up in a panic with similar sensations.

I would like to tell you Debbie's story. I prayed for Debbie, who was feeling desperate. She had a low self-image and was constantly gripped with feelings of loneliness. She was an only child and was caught up in making her own identity, as she didn't know who she was.

As I prayed, I asked Debbie to think of herself in a safe place when she was a child. Nothing seemed to be happening, so I asked her, 'Where did you go to when you wanted to feel safe?' Suddenly she sobbed and sobbed, and said that there was nowhere that ever felt safe. This surprised me, as Debbie had told me that she came from a loving family home.

After a little while I asked her to see herself or think of herself in her back garden at home. I asked her to open the back door (as she didn't have a gate into the garden) so that she could allow Jesus to come and be in the garden with her. She started to cry a lot, and was also shaking. She didn't know where she was. I asked her what was happening. She said that as she opened the back door to her house, an incredible loneliness hit her. Debbie started getting really worked up as she began to describe how she had always felt she would die at a young age, as if it were inevitable. She was convinced of this, and this fear often gripped her.

Earlier on, when we had first spoken together, she said

she had an idea that her mum might have had an earlier miscarriage, although her mother had never told her this – it was more an impression that her mother's womb wasn't a safe place for her. I now asked if I could pray for her as a tiny baby in the womb, and she said 'yes'.

As I started to pray, she was shaking slightly – trembling like a scared little thing. Then the most beautiful ministry took place. I invited Father God to come and put his hands on her in the womb; I asked for Jesus to shine the light of his love to make that womb feel a safe place to be. I prayed about the fear of death: I bound it and loosed it and broke the power of it in Jesus' name, and told it to go into the hands of Jesus. Then I prayed in the life of Jesus, the abundant life, his promise to her, and for a safe delivery of her as a baby – especially through the birth canal. In Jesus' name, I encouraged this little baby into the world.

Later, she said it was incredible: she had felt as if she was passing through a very narrow place. All the time she said she felt all the fear go and she felt safe. She experienced being a little baby, just born, and felt the heat of Jesus' body as he held her. She said this was the first time anything like this had ever happened to her.

In Jesus' name, I cut her off from the fear coming from her mother and from the chemicals released by that fear that Debbie had received via the umbilical cord.

A week later, Debbie told me that she had spoken to her mother about her birth and discovered that her mother had indeed had a miscarriage during her previous pregnancy. She had been very frightened when Debbie was in the womb and during her birth. Her biggest fear had been that Debbie would die.

Isn't it wonderful what our Jesus does? Debbie experienced the healing of her memories as well as the healing of her emotions.

We don't need healing from everything we have suffered, but some things have given us pain and caused us to shut down emotionally.

Some of us were told at an early age that we were not wanted. We were told that we were 'mistakes'.

I remember when I was young, about eight years old, I was walking along with my mum, dad and brother eating an ice-cream cone, and the scene is etched in my memory. I was talking with my mum and don't remember the conversation beforehand, but the words that came next pierced me right to my soul.

My mum said, 'Of course we didn't want you – we couldn't afford you, you were the last thing we wanted right then.'

To justify it now I could say, 'They were poor, they already had my six-month-old baby brother. It must have been a shock when my mum became pregnant again. She was anxious and mentally ill.' But for the little girl who heard that she wasn't wanted, it was an enormous blow. It was as if something entered me that day, and that something was rejection.

From the moment that I realised I wasn't a wanted child, it had a big effect on me. I didn't feel worth much, I wasn't wanted. Some people who hear things like this have no reaction, as they know that they are loved. For me, though, it made a big difference. From then on I had the feeling that if people knew me they wouldn't really like me. It also made me feel lonely.

For some of us, being in the womb was a scary place. For others it was a safe place, but we were scared to leave it.

Something that brought about a measure of healing for me was Psalm 139. This is my favourite psalm. It says, 'My frame was not hidden from you when I was made in the secret place' (v. 15). Isaiah and Jeremiah both said that God called them 'from the womb'. Almighty God, Father God, was there at all of our beginnings, at our conception. We were made because *he* said so. He was the one who gave us life. Again in Psalm 139 it says, 'All the days ordained for me were written in your book before one of them came to be' (v. 16).

I found it helpful to know that although I was conceived because of failed contraception, all the days of my life were already ordained by God before one of them even happened! I was no mistake to God. God called us into being in the same way that he called all life into being. We are made in his image for his pleasure. He takes great delight in knowing that he made you, and he delights in the fact that he made me. That makes me feel more than just wanted. It makes me feel cherished. Knowing that I am cherished has brought me healing. When I read Psalm 139, I read it as truth: I know that I belong and it makes me feel safe. I am known, I was wanted. As it says in Genesis 2, God looked at all that he had made, and he 'saw that it was good' (v. 25). God makes good things, not 'mistakes'. The good news, as Genesis tells us, is that after God made the animals, he saw that it was good, but after he made man, he saw that it was '*very* good'. What a great thing to celebrate!

After I became a Christian, I became aware that I was

afraid of dying – it would make me feel panicky. I asked Jesus to surface anything that needed healing. One day in church I thought about my birth, which had been quite traumatic. At about the same time I also learned that as a small child I had been rushed to hospital with severe delayed concussion and had nearly died. A priest had sat by my bed all night and gave me the last rites, but miraculously I lived. My mother often told me that as I was being born she had a vision of Jesus at the end of the bed. She almost died having me. So it would seem that death played a bit of a role in my life as a child. Death came close on more than one occasion.

I explained these things to a friend called Margaret. She started to pray for me. I recalled what my mother had told me of my birth and suddenly had a picture of my mother in labour. Suddenly I was aware of a black shadowy figure by the bed. It was quite overwhelming and made me feel as if I was gasping for breath. Margaret prayed a prayer of deliverance for me and broke the power of death in Jesus' name. She spoke the life of Jesus into me. I felt an immediate release and haven't suffered in the same way since.

Let's pray

Let's just shut our eyes.

Holy Spirit, I receive you now. Father, you saw us in the womb. I open myself up to you now. Come into my memories of me as that little baby, that foetus.

In the Bible it says, 'Before I formed you in the womb I knew you' (Jeremiah 1:5). In Genesis 1:31 we read, 'God saw all that he had made, and it was very good.' God was pleased that he made you.

Allow Jesus to come and visit you when you were in your mother's womb.

Father God, please lay your hands on what you made.

You were ordained by him to be born (see Psalm 139:16). Let Jesus deliver you now as that baby. Trust him to take you through that experience, that trauma. For those traumatised by the birth, be free now in Jesus' name. Be at peace and know that he was with you.

Don't struggle. Those who couldn't breathe during the birth, now breathe in the power of the Holy Spirit.

Breathe on them, Jesus, with your breath.

Jesus is the same yesterday, today and for ever, and he can come and visit our yesterdays.

Lord Jesus, come. Amen.

You may find it helpful to ask someone to pray with you about any traumatic birth experience that you may have recalled as you read this chapter.

Becky had been sexually abused as a baby by her father. This continued for years throughout her childhood, and others also abused her in various ways, especially emotionally. Her father was imprisoned for the abuse and her parents divorced. As you can imagine, Becky's self-worth and self-esteem were very low when I met her and she felt disgusted at herself. After several sessions Becky started to get healed up. It was a long road as Jesus met with her in her pain and agony.

One day we were discussing Becky's desire to articulate her feelings, as she seemed to go around in circles trying to make sense of her horror story. She was tortured by guilt, as most people who have been abused usually are. All she ever wanted was to be loved and this was something that she had never experienced. She had a good relationship with Jesus, but didn't really know God that well as her Father. Then Becky realised that the child within her had suffered such a lack of affection and, in fact, a lack of anything good, as well as feelings of never really belonging anywhere. She had always felt as if no one ever wanted her – as if she never really had a home.

During a prayer time she allowed these feelings to surface and invited Jesus to come and heal these deep-rooted feelings of abandonment. Jesus came and showed her a house full of little children. She went into the house and joined them, playing and belonging. I had no idea what she was seeing, but at that same moment I quoted a verse from Scripture out loud: 'In my Father's house are many rooms . . . I am going there to prepare a place for you' (John 14:2). I suddenly thought, 'This sounds like a funeral, like a death.' I sensed Jesus saying, 'Yes, a death of what was.' I waited and prayed in silence, allowing Jesus to do what he wanted to do. Tears flowed down my face as I sensed his healing presence and his love and compassion for that little girl.

After a while, I shared a picture that I had seen. At the

doorway stood a man with Becky as a little girl dressed beautifully, as if at a royal ceremony. The man announced in a very loud voice, 'Here is Becky – she belongs to Jesus, she belongs to Father God.' Then I saw her dressed as a princess. Again the man announced to everyone present, 'Here is Becky, daughter of the King.'

He pierced the depths of her suffering with that identity. No words could do that, only the powerful love of the one who called her to himself.

Becky cried and cried as she received her very identity from the King himself. He acknowledged her as belonging. It was as if the angels were announcing Becky's identity in the spiritual realm as well as the earthly one. It was a holy moment. She belongs to the King, she belongs to Jesus, and she is his. Becky held her hands on her chest as she received this realisation, as she received it into the depths of her being. It was beautiful to watch such a healing.

Afterwards she said that she realised she would never be the same again. It was a life-changing thing for her. Becky knew that God had given her a place to visit again and again, that place of belonging. She said she knew that when she got into bed every night she could surrender herself to the one who would comfort her, who would visit her to say 'goodnight'. Now she would have all the things she had never experienced as a little girl. Thank you, Jesus, you do all things well.

We all have the potential for being the way the Lord made us to be, but circumstances beyond our control can stunt our growth. When bad things happen to us when we are young, they have the potential to become stumbling blocks to us. This means that when we grow up, we don't have a choice about our reactions as we are locked into a response based on our past experience. Sometimes we are locked into a pattern or cycle of behaviour. What happens in inner healing is that we ask Jesus in by the power of the Holy Spirit. We co-operate with what the Holy Spirit is showing us. We choose to change, to forgive or let go of past experiences and pain. We let him break cycles or patterns of behaviour.

The Bible tells us that Jesus is the same yesterday, today and for ever, so we can invite Jesus to come into our yesterdays. Time is not a barrier to him; he can visit our memories, if we give him permission to do so.

Psychologists say that memories and feelings are locked away at the same time; we don't have a memory locked away without the feelings of that time. Did you know that smells and tastes are also locked away in our memories? If I smell newly laid Tarmac, I am immediately transported back to a hot summer afternoon in my childhood, when I was about ten years old. I can even remember exactly where I was standing. I lived on a massive council estate in Dagenham and nothing ever happened there that was exciting. Except for this day, when the pavements were being resurfaced. I remember the delicious-smelling black stuff on the pavement and the delight of watching my shoes sinking into it!

I once saw a television programme in which they experimented with taste. People were given some unusual foods. Some of these foods they hadn't tasted for as long as 60 years, but they knew what they were. They gave some people dried egg, and immediately it hit their tastebuds it released memories of the Second World War. Some of them didn't know what it was they were tasting, but memories and associations were released. This proved that memories and tastes were definitely linked.

Mary Pytches has written a lot of excellent books, and one of them is called *Yesterday's Child*. We all have yesterday's child within us, and for some of us that child is locked away inside us with all the shame, anger, disappointment and rejection. We deny it and lock it away. This is often referred to as the 'inner child'. We can judge this 'inner child', and maybe we don't like this child with all those big emotions of anger and hatred. Maybe we're ashamed of this part of ourselves, this part that has never been allowed to grow up. We can then cut ourselves off and reject this 'inner child'. Because this part of ourselves never grows up, it is an immature part of us. Sometimes, though, this part of us seeps through.

Philippians 2:12–13 says, 'Continue to work out your salvation with fear and trembling, for it is God who works in you to will and to act according to his good purpose.' This again is talking about wholeness, about making whole our body, mind and spirit. This verse says that God will work in you, but it also says you must work out your salvation, your wholeness. We have to take responsibility with God alongside us.

People who are very locked away with their inner child can be very introverted. They can be control freaks, and they tend to marry people who are extroverts. They love to see their freedom. They long for it themselves, but cannot attain it. The trouble is, they then spend the rest of their lives trying to control their partner. This is, of course, impossible.

Mary Pytches was telling me that she struggled with the inner child thing and didn't really understand it until she had a dream. In the dream, she was getting married and had two bridesmaids. One was beautiful, the other was bedraggled and disgusting. In the dream she said, 'Will someone please do something about this disgusting child?' She realised she had to do something herself; she had to take responsibility. The disgusting child was how she saw herself. When she awoke, she realised that *she* was the one who could do something about this. She had to choose to take the lid off and allow this 'yesterday's child' to get healed up.

The Bible is full of people who were healed by God. In the New Testament Jesus often used a little phrase, which was a spiritual gift, a word of knowledge or a word of wisdom, to show that he knew about the person's past life. He did such a thing to a little man called Zacchaeus. Jesus saw Zacchaeus up a tree; he was trying to get a better view of Jesus. Out of all the things he could have said to Zacchaeus, I am astounded at what he chose to say to him. Zacchaeus was a tax collector and cheated people out of money, but Jesus ignored all this and said to him, 'I am coming to your house for tea.' These words had a profound effect on Zacchaeus. I believe these words brought healing to him. I think that as a little boy, Zacchaeus didn't have anyone coming to his house for tea. I think he was either too afraid to let them come and see what his home life was like, or else he didn't have any friends. Maybe he was bullied as a child because he was small for his age; maybe he was lonely and isolated. Maybe this led to him becoming aggressive towards others, trying to get back at people for hurting him. We will never know, but one thing is for sure: Jesus in his mercy looked past the sin of Zacchaeus to see its cause, and he addressed it. He visited the inner child of Zacchaeus with these words, 'I am coming to your house for tea.' Zacchaeus was healed and gave back even more money than he had taken.

I met someone once in South Africa who also needed Jesus to visit that 'inner child'. Ellen had been repeatedly sexually abused as a child. My friend and I spoke to her at length to find out what issues she had already dealt with. She was what I would term a prickly-pear sort of person. On the outside she wasn't very approachable, but on the inside she was soft. She had received prayer ministry in the past, but hadn't seen much change in her life. She said she felt abnormal, but longed to know Jesus close to her; she so wanted to change and feel normal. After some prayer we saw that her 'inner child' had not been allowed to express the pain of her abuse. We chatted some more and then continued to minister the power and love of Jesus. At one point she almost stopped the ministry as her inner pain started to surface. Suddenly she realised that the 'inner child' part of herself with all that pain was locked away as if inside a cupboard. She had an image of herself as a child locked inside and as an adult not allowing the child to get out. Ellen battled with this as she realised that this had been the stumbling block in her life, especially in the area of relationships. Just as she was not letting this inner child out, so she also never allowed anyone to get close to her. At last she chose to let her inner child express herself. She cried and cried – such an agonising cry. Tears of pain and abuse, of humiliation and agony, of despair and degradation. It was painful to watch, but then beautiful as we saw her changing before our eyes. It was beautiful to see the compassion and tenderness of Jesus reflected in Ellen's face. Ellen forgave herself and embraced that part of herself that she had previously rejected.

After the ministry Ellen kept saying over and over, 'I'm OK, I really am OK now.' We asked her what she meant, and she said that now she felt like a normal person – like other people, not abnormal any more.

The next day when we saw her we were amazed to see her dressed in bright clothes, with her hair styled in a different way. She looked years younger. We went to chat to her and she said that when she told her pastor husband what had happened the previous day, he cried. He had longed for her healing to take place for many years. Then he said he now had a new wife: he had never seen her so free before. We left them, and as we turned back we saw Ellen spontaneously fling her arms around her husband and hug him in front of everyone. From what she had previously said, we knew that for Ellen this was a completely new thing to do. Thank you, Jesus, you did it again!

So how can we get healed from cutting ourselves off from our inner child? The first step is to recognise that we need to do something. The second step is to confess it to God: 'I am sorry, Jesus, that I have cut myself off or have rejected part of myself. . .' The third step is to receive forgiveness and forgive ourselves. The fourth step is to choose to embrace instead of reject that part of yourself which suffered the abuse or pain in the first place.

Let's pray

Please come, Holy Spirit. (Let's give the Holy Spirit access to our inner child, yesterday's child, the child who didn't express the pain, rejection and abuse. Allow Jesus to come and visit the child within – give him permission.) *Jesus, I am sorry I have locked part of myself away. Please forgive me – thank you that you do, Lord, I receive it. In your name, Jesus, I choose now to allow that part of me, my inner child, to live.* (Now say to your inner child, 'I allow you to express what you didn't express in the past. I am sorry that I rejected you and was ashamed of you. [Add anything else that is appropriate to you.] I now allow you to grow up.' You may find it helpful to imagine yourself as a young boy/girl in a room. Then see yourself as an adult walking into that room and embracing that small child. Ask for his/her forgiveness. As a child, embrace the adult.) *Thank you, Jesus. Amen.*

I have seen a lot of very special healing times taking place regarding the 'inner child'. The terminology may seem strange to you, but don't let that put you off availing yourself of this type of prayer ministry. The love of Jesus is so amazing, deep and precious.

There are some things that are not straightforward to explain regarding inner healing, as Jesus brings the healing in so many different ways. To illustrate this, I thought I would tell you some stories of what I have seen Jesus do in my own life and in the lives of others to bring deep and lasting healing. Often when we read about what Jesus has done in someone's life, it can open us up to receive what he wants to do for us. Be aware, though, that he will probably do it in a completely different way for you, because you are a different person, unique in every way.

When I was pregnant with our third child, I was driving along a country lane when my five-year-old daughter Alex asked, 'Mummy, was I your first baby?' I nearly crashed the car up the bank with surprise at such a question and it felt as if all the blood had drained out of my body. I had never told Alex that I had given birth to a stillborn child, and we had never talked about this in our family since she was born.

I took a deep breath and said, 'No, darling, Mummy had another little girl born before you.'

Excitedly she asked, 'What's her name?'

Suddenly I had a strange sensation in my head – as if two halves of my head suddenly came together – as I uttered the name that had never been uttered, the name that had been chosen for her: 'Sarah, her name is Sarah.'

I felt an amazing joy and relief flooding my body. My baby's name was Sarah; she was part of our family, not a stillborn any longer, but a child with a name. Alex didn't stop talking about Sarah for the whole journey. She included Sarah in our family life; she was so excited that she had a sister. During the next few weeks, whenever we were talking about family things the name of Sarah was popped in as belonging to us. Relatives started asking, 'Who is this Sarah you keep mentioning?' With great pleasure, Alex told everyone about her baby sister who was now in heaven with Jesus.

This was such a healing time for us all. For me the healing was instantaneous, as I spoke Sarah's name. I was so thankful to Jesus for using our own daughter to bring about this healing in my life. As you can see, the healing I received that day also affected the rest of our family.

The question Alex asked – 'Was I your first baby?' – was something that is referred to in the Bible as a word of knowledge. There was no natural reason for her to have asked such a question. When I heard it, I felt as if all the blood drained from my body – it was such an unusual thing for a five-year-old to say. I knew it was something supernatural, but I couldn't understand it. Often it's like that with healing: we don't always understand it, because God is mighty and huge. Why would we understand it? The Bible tells us that God says, 'My ways are not your ways,' and, 'My thoughts are not your thoughts.' He is so much bigger than we could ever imagine.

That word of knowledge was like the time when Jesus told the woman at the well, 'Go, call your husband and come back.'

She replied, 'I have no husband.'

Jesus then said, 'You are right when you say you have no husband. The fact is, you have had five husbands, and the man you now have is not your husband.'

This woman had looked for a man to satisfy her needs, but obviously hadn't found him! The woman told people that Jesus knew 'everything I ever did' (the story is told in John 4:1–42). Sometimes healing is like that. Jesus shows us one thing after another, all connected to a deep inner need. In this woman's case, I suspect her need was for unconditional love, and that's why she had so many hus-bands. The great thing was that Jesus healed her and saved her all in one go!

I met a girl named Carly in South Africa and learned during several prayer ministry times that she had been sexually, physically and emotionally abused. During one prayer time she remembered her grandfather sexually abusing her and then standing in the doorway of the bedroom. He was looking menacing and Carly felt scared and powerless. Into my mind came the verses in Ephesians 6 about being clothed with the armour of God. I told Carly what the scripture said and what it means, then told her, 'Put on the armour of God and tell him to get out.' Instead of being scared, Carly needed to exercise the authority in Jesus' name which is given to every believer.

She did this, and the image changed. Suddenly she saw herself as a child in a dark room. She knew her grandfather was outside guarding the door. She then saw Jesus in this memory in her 'yesterday'. Dressed in the armour of God, she told her grandfather to go away. She told him out loud that what he had done was wrong and she told him how it made her feel. At last she had courage and a voice. She then forgave him and he left the memory.

Then Carly saw herself scrubbing the bed, saying over and over, 'So dirty, so dirty.' I said to her, 'Allow Jesus to lie on that bed.' She did allow him, although it made her cry fiercely. I then asked Jesus to do what he wanted to do and carried on praying in the Spirit. Later she said that Jesus had picked her up and taken her out into the garden. Jesus then started to burn the bed. Next she was outside in the sunshine with Jesus.

Carly then forgave the little girl inside herself who repulsed her, and she laid down the big stick she beat herself up with – usually critical words. At the end of the ministry time, she said she knew that she was really loved and felt free at last.

We can see that during that time of healing it was good to use Scripture. It's powerful and we're meant to use it as a weapon, especially when we feel powerless. 'The word of God is . . . sharper than any double-edged sword' (Hebrews 4:12).

We don't just need to use the words, however: we also need to understand what they mean. I've heard Christians say, 'Oh, I never go out without the armour of God on. I say it every day.' It's not a superstitious thing, it's about knowing the truth of what we've been given for our protection and applying it. We need to know that we're clothed with the armour of God and that at times we need to stand firm with it on against all the schemes of the evil one, against anything that comes against us. As we saw, we can also use it when looking into our past hurts like Carly did, so that we can face the pain and not be afraid.

It's wonderful seeing Jesus heal children of frightening things. When our youngest daughter Beth was eight years old, she was very insecure and frightened of her teacher. One evening when she was in bed, I asked her to shut her eyes and remember her classroom, to see herself there. Then I said, 'Go to the door of the classroom and ask Jesus to come in.' I then just prayed quietly in tongues.

Afterwards she said that Jesus went and stood next to her teacher. Beth said that she went to sit in her usual seat and watched Jesus and the teacher. It was so lovely watching the expressions changing on Beth's face. Beth then said that she went up to Jesus without fear and he took her back to her seat and sat her on his lap. As Beth lay in bed, I saw her arms started to move around and she said she was cuddling Jesus. Jesus then took her all around the classroom. Later she said Jesus took her to all the other places in her school that she was scared of. I carried on praying quietly, not saying anything to her.

Beth then said that she could see herself in the hallway of our house. She went through the motions of opening a door. Next she said that Jesus was coming with her up to her bedroom and he was tucking her up in bed. Then I asked her, 'Do you want Jesus to go anywhere else?' Suddenly her face lit up and she said that Jesus was going to the other side of her bed where it was dark near the window, where she was always scared burglars would come. She said that Jesus made it all bright everywhere, even under the bed, and she wasn't scared any more. Next she was smiling and nodding.

Later on, while wiping the tears from my eyes, I asked her what had happened. Beth said that Jesus had come back to her bedside and said to her that she didn't have to be scared any more, because he was looking after her and would always be in her bedroom with her when she was asleep. The next day she went happily to school and lost all her fear of the teacher.

We don't have to do it – we allow Jesus to come into things and go with what he is doing. We must *never* suggest things to children in prayer ministry, as they are very vulnerable and we want Jesus to do the healing ministry, not us!

We don't have to be afraid about the Lord using our imagination – he made it for us to use, so we can turn it over to him.

A lot of children use fantasy as a switch-off from reality, like daydreaming or having an imaginary friend. Children do this type of thing a lot if they're lonely or unhappy. As we get older, we may need to be released from this, as it can be a habit in our life. Just ask the Holy Spirit to come and cleanse your imagination and any fantasy in your life. Dedicate your imagination to Jesus.

During another time of praying with Carly, she told me that she was petrified of men. As she had been physically, sexually and emotionally abused by them, this was hardly surprising. As I prayed and ministered the love of Jesus to her, I realised that it was probably difficult for Carly to relate in a deep way to Jesus, because of him coming to earth as a man. I asked her if this posed a problem for her, and she said that yes it did. Then I thought, 'Oh no, how are you going to get round this one, Lord?'

An answer came back immediately: of course Jesus didn't come to earth as a man, but as a baby!

Then I said to Carly, 'Do you think you could come and meet Jesus as a tiny baby in the stable?'

She agreed. After a little while, she started to weep and then she smiled. I asked her what was happening and she said that Jesus as a baby was holding her little finger.

I then said to her, 'Do you think you could receive Jesus as a baby?'

She said, 'Yes.'

Well, it was no good her having an intimate relationship with baby Jesus all her life – things needed to move on! So I used my common sense and said, 'Do you think you could meet Jesus now as a little boy?'

She agreed, and once more tears flowed down her face and after a while she smiled again.

'What happened this time?' I asked.

'Jesus was holding my hand and we were running through fields,' she replied.

Again I asked her, 'Could you receive Jesus the little boy?'

'Yes,' she said.

Now I was really getting the hang of it, so I said, 'Carly, how about meeting Jesus now as a teenager?'

Once more came the same pattern of tears and then smiling. I could hardly wait. 'What now?' I asked eagerly.

She said, 'Jesus is giving me flowers that he picked for me.'

At this point my own tears started to flow. How wonderful of Jesus – of course, just the right thing for a young lady to receive!

At last I thought she was ready. 'Carly, do you think you could now receive Jesus the Son of Man, the Son of God?'

'Yes!' she said wholeheartedly, with a big smile on her face.

We never did pray about her fear of men, but the next day she came running up to me to report the good news. In one of the main meetings, Mike Pilavachi, leading from the stage, had asked all the young people to hold hands for some light-hearted fun and it wasn't until later that Carly realised she had been holding the hand of a young man. Before that day, Carly had been terrified even by the smell of a man's aftershave, let alone the idea of holding a man's hand. Thank you, Jesus, for such a restoring healing.

From this we can also see how creative God is. Of course

he's creative, he made the world! He created us, he isn't in time, and he can step back into our memories and be there. He can create scenarios that he can use to bring healing to us. He can release feelings that were never expressed.

Some of us may feel so hurt that God *allowed* what happened to us. It causes us pain when we think things like, 'Why didn't you stop what was happening?' or, 'Where were you then, Jesus?' These are valid questions, but they show us that we're actually blaming God for what happened. We know God is powerful; why then does it seem as if God became powerless to stop what was happening to us?

First of all, we need to acknowledge that God does care about us. He does love us, he wasn't angry with us, neither was he too busy to bother with us or stop what was happening to us. We have to remember what God actually did. He gave up being able to do everything and be everywhere at the same time and gave up his divine attributes to come to earth to be a vulnerable little baby. In fact, he arrived in such a way as to be completely powerless. He became the baby of a teenager who was poor. He was born into filthy conditions. People wanted him dead before he had even learned to speak properly. Jesus came to be fully human. He also subjected himself to be terribly abused without his Father there to protect him. God can understand powerlessness. He chose this way, to be human and to suffer and to die, even though humankind had chosen to live without him. He gave us the power to choose. God chose not to rescue us supernaturally from our abusers, so that our abusers also could have that same freedom to choose good or evil. Jesus endured abuse for our sake and for our abusers' sake. We have a choice: to blame God for what happened, or to blame the Fall and man's sin and the evil that is in the world.

There is no easy answer here, but you need to realise that Jesus was weeping as he watched what happened to you. He wants to come now and share in that suffering, to enter that time and heal you from it.

I have read in various books that Jesus does not heal memories. I know this is not true, because Jesus has done that for me and for others with whom I have prayed. He doesn't have to heal a memory to bring healing, however. Also, we don't have to recall memories of abuse for Jesus to heal us. For some of us it would be the worst thing to remember such horrors.

Some of the stories of healing I've shared with you concern pain that no psychiatrist or doctor or counsellor could heal. These stories may be able to point out to you where you need healing, but only God can heal.

Jesus heals with such tenderness, compassion and beauty. Jesus uses doctors, nurses and therapists, and also medicines when we're sick. He shows researchers the way forward and reveals how to heal diseases. But he also does healing in supernatural ways.

The Bible tells us that 'our eyes are the light to our soul'. This means that whatever acts our eyes have seen – evil acts, sexual images, pornography, physical abuse, sexual abuse, repeated drunkenness – need cleansing. If you have willingly done these things, ask for forgiveness, turn away from them.

Let's pray now for that.

Let's pray

I am so sorry, Lord, for . . .

Please forgive me. I turn away from that now.

Please come and cleanse me, Jesus – cleanse my eyes, cleanse my body, cleanse my mind. With the light of your love, shine into my soul. I dedicate my body to you.

If you saw any of the evil acts I mentioned, or any were done to you, if you have images etched in your mind, do the same thing: ask Jesus for cleansing of your eyes, your mind, your body. Dedicate your body to Jesus.

The Bible says we are to offer our bodies as instruments of worship. If you are a self-harmer (if you cut yourself, hit or scratch yourself, pull hair out or practise self-abuse), then confess that to Jesus now. Allow him to surface the pain that you have been covering up. Trust him now.

> You've kept track of my every toss and turn
> > through the sleepless nights,
> Each tear entered in your ledger,
> > each ache written in your book. (Psalm 56:8, *The Message*)

I find that very comforting. I want to finish this chapter with a very personal story. I've only told it a few times, because it's very precious to me and so I don't tell it casually. I tell it to you in the hope that it will glorify Jesus. Only he, the lover of my soul, could have done such a thing.

A few years after our two-year-old daughter Joanna drowned, I was visiting a friend's daughter in hospital. She had just had major heart surgery. She lay in intensive care, naked, with tubes attached all over her body. As I looked at her, I rushed from the room feeling faint. I sat on the floor, my head swimming with memories of my own daughter lying on a hospital emergency bed, as the doctors fought to save her life. I soon left the hospital with the memory that had plagued me for years going around in my head. A couple of weeks later, I visited someone else in hospital. This time it was a teenager who was in the children's ward suffering from a badly broken leg. As I sat by the bed, another child was brought back from theatre. As I looked over at the child, a piece of sheet moved to reveal a tube going into the child's naked body. Again I felt faint and the image of my own naked child with tubes attached filled my mind.

I quickly excused myself and left the hospital. These memories were really shouting at me now and I realised I had to do something about them. The following week at church, I went up to the front for prayer and a group of keen prayers surrounded me (our model of ministry is actually two people praying, at the most three). Initially the memory of Joanna fighting for life was in my mind, but as soon as they started to pray, I fell to the floor and nothing else happened. Within seconds I was able to open my eyes and actually wanted to go home. The problem was, they were still praying earnestly. I didn't want to seem a spoilsport, so I lay there a while longer as they seemed to be enjoying themselves. At last I said, 'Sorry, but everything has gone cold and these memories are no longer available to me.' My friend Mary said I was not to worry – they would soon come back when they were ripe and ready for healing. She said I was to ring her as soon as everything resurfaced, and she and another friend called Margaret would pray with me.

The next day, as soon as I woke up, I started to have lots of memories about my mother. 'Oh no,' I thought. 'This is the last thing I want!' Throughout the day I got more and more angry as memories of how much my mother had let me down worked me up into a frenzy. By the evening my head was about to burst. I was so upset and so angry at how my mother had treated me. I rang Mary, and she arranged to meet me with Margaret at the church.

After chatting about what had happened that day, they started to pray and ask the Holy Spirit to come upon me in power. After a while, they said I now needed to forgive my mother. After I'd said 'I can't' a few times, they pointed out that it was a command of God, not a feeling. They told me that I needed to confess my anger and hatred of my mother to the Lord and ask for forgiveness, and with the forgiveness that I received I was to forgive my mother. Almost through clenched teeth, I forgave my mother.

All the anger went. I then realised what had prompted all this. Because I'd judged my own mother as letting me down, I'd always felt that I'd let Joanna down by allowing her to fall into the swimming pool. Then I knew that all this was in the way of my own healing. I told Mary and Margaret that I now felt ready to remember the images that struck horror into my soul.

As they prayed, I had a sense of thick blackness engulfing me. It was terrifying. I felt as if I was being almost suffocated by it. With my will, I started to push through it. With my will, I said that I wanted to see that memory again. I didn't want it to hold me in fear any longer. Suddenly a door opened and there I was, seeing the scene vividly, as if it was happening for the first time. I said to Mary and Margaret, 'I can see it; I'm there again.'

Mary said, 'Look for Jesus. He is there. Just look for him.'

At first I felt panicky, trying to work Jesus up, trying to make it happen. But then I realised I didn't have to do that: he was willing to be there, he wanted to be there. I relaxed a bit more and in my head asked him to be there with me. What happened next was supernatural.

Suddenly the whole scene changed, and instead of me standing there looking at Joanna's head, the memory changed and I was looking at her naked body from the feet up. I saw hands dipping into a jar of sweet-smelling ointment (I knew it was the same stuff mentioned in the Bible – 'pure nard', an expensive embalming ointment). These hands were spreading the beautiful ointment all over Joanna's body. Jesus was saying to me, 'I am preparing her for her burial.'

The impact of these words reduced me to an indescribable and incredulous joy. Over and over, out loud, I kept saying, 'But I thought that was for you. How can this be? I thought this was for you. I didn't know that you would do this for her.' Mary said later that for half an hour, with tears streaming down my face, I repeated these same words. I couldn't believe that my Jesus, who was anointed by a woman in the Bible with costly perfume, was now doing the same thing for my child. To me this would have been a blasphemous thing if someone else had told me such a story.

These images have stayed with me as clearly as I saw them when I first received this healing. These images and this memory still reduce me to tears. As I type these words, I still cannot comprehend a more beautiful way to change such a horrific memory into one that is so beautiful. The old memory haunted me and spoke over and over of death, trauma and agony. This healed memory is one that I revisited for years, and each time it blessed me and healed me a bit more. That my Lord and King would do such a thing for me is beyond words. That he would stoop down and do such a thing for a little child is incredible. But this is what he said: 'Let the little children come to me, and do not hinder them, for the kingdom of heaven belongs to such as these' (Matthew 19:14).

EXERCISES

Negative tapes from the past can play in our head. We need to recognise what these are, renounce those that we have believed to be true and then replace them with the truth.

Start to recognise these phrases that play in your head throughout the next few weeks. As you start to realise what they are, replace them with the truth of Scripture. Replace these negative tapes with the truth.

> If you hold to my teaching . . . you will know the truth, and the truth will set you free. (John 8:31–32)

Negative tape: *You are worthless.*

Truth: The Bible shows us what we are worth. We are worth dying for.

> For God so loved the world that he gave his one and only Son, that whoever believes in him shall not perish but have eternal life. (John 3:16)

Negative tape: *If people really knew me they wouldn't like me.*
Truth: The Bible shows us that we are known personally.

> Are not two sparrows sold for a penny? Yet not one of them will fall to the ground apart from the will of your Father. And even the very hairs of your head are all numbered. So don't be afraid; you are worth more than many sparrows. (Matthew 10:29–31)

Negative tape: *You are stupid.*
Truth: Read the whole passage of 1 Corinthians 1:18–31 and 1 Corinthians 2.

Now fill out your own 'negative tapes' below and find a corresponding verse to give you the truth. A concordance or online Bible will help you search for a suitable verse.

Negative tape: *You are. . .*
Truth:

Negative tape: *You are. . .*
Truth:

At first these verses will just sound like words, but each time the negative tape plays in your head, say the verse out loud. After a while, you will see that the truth will start planting itself in your mind as you take it on and proclaim it.

Pick out the exercises below that seem relevant to you.

- If you recall being scared about going home after school because of what you might find at home, take time to ask Jesus to walk home with you. Ask him to come and visit that little boy or little girl who walked home every day uncertain. Read about the disciples who were anxious and worried after Jesus' death, walking on the road to Emmaus (Luke 24). Imagine that scene and walk along as an adult with them. Let Jesus meet with you.
- Read Psalm 23, about Jesus the Shepherd. Use that psalm to meditate on Jesus the Shepherd looking after the lambs. 'I will fear no evil . . . your rod and your staff, they comfort me.'
- Ask the Holy Spirit, the Comforter, to come to the little boy or little girl inside who was lonely. Tell Jesus how you feel. Ask Jesus to come and be your friend.
- If you have any recurrent dreams, ask Jesus what they relate to. Keep a journal – write prayers in it and let Jesus speak to you in reply. Actively seek healing for things that come up.
- If any memories come back to you, write them down and see if there is a pattern. Ask Jesus to come to the root memory. Ask him to visit your yesterdays and bring his healing power. Take time to do this, taking one memory at a time. If this is really painful, get someone else to support you in prayer while you face the pain.
- Even though memories contain hurt done to you, take responsibility for your reactions that need repentance and forgiveness from Jesus.
- If you find it difficult to visualise memories, recall to

mind things you liked doing as a child. Ask Jesus to come and visit you, sharing these activities with you. Give him permission to do what he wants, to heal you of past hurt.

• Read Isaiah 61. First of all, ask the Holy Spirit to come and ask him to show you any part that relates to you. Turn it into prayer.

• Read about people Jesus met, think about what they must have suffered and see which of them you relate to. Put yourself in that scene and let Jesus speak to you.

Although we receive healing in the past, we need to take responsibility to make a difference in the present. We may have to change our patterns of behaviour and commit to change.

SCRIPTURES

• Concerning creative prayer: we can ask Jesus to enter our yesterday in order to heal, and he does, but we can also see by faith, as in Hebrews 11.

• As it says in Romans 4:17, he is 'the God who gives life to the dead and calls things that are not as though they were'.

• Read the whole of John 17, where Jesus prays to the Father about us.

• Here is an encouraging verse: 'Now the Lord is the Spirit, and where the Spirit of the Lord is, there is freedom' (2 Corinthians 3:17).

• Psalm 56:8 says, 'List my tears on your scroll – are they not in your record?'

• In 2 Kings 20:5 we read, 'This is what the LORD, the God

of your father David, says: I have heard your prayer and seen your tears; I will heal you.'

- Daniel 2:22 tells us, 'He reveals deep and hidden things; he knows what lies in darkness, and light dwells with him.'

- And finally, in Psalm 91:14–16 we read, 'Because he loves me . . . I will rescue him; I will protect him, for he acknowledges my name. He will call upon me, and I will answer him; I will be with him in trouble, I will deliver him and honour him. With long life will I satisfy him and show him my salvation.'

5: **Breaking Vows and Oaths**

As we grew up, we were taught by our parents or carers about things that could harm us:

- Don't touch the cooker – you'll be burned.
- Don't play on the motorway – you'll get killed.
- Don't accept sweets from strangers.

These instructions were for our safety and our protection. This was good teaching, but none of us has perfect parents, so they also taught us things that weren't helpful and we believed those things too.

Some beliefs we have are things that we were taught or that we caught from our parents, or they're beliefs that we chose because something bad happened to us. Some of these beliefs are called irrational beliefs. For example: 'Don't tread on the cracks in the pavement – you'll go blind.' I'm sure we would all agree that this is an irrational belief.

But how about this one? 'It's wrong to need other people.' What happens if that's your belief and then you need help? Do you just grit your teeth and struggle on?

My husband Ken was bedridden in hospital for five weeks. He had an infection in his spine and needed 24-hour care. When he came home, he needed nursing for the next six months, as he couldn't stand or sit. What if that had been his irrational belief, that he didn't need people? What would have happened to him? The answer to that one is that he would have died!

I remember when I had an operation and, unknown to me, all the muscles in my stomach region had gone into spasm. I was in agony, taking 14 tablets a day, and still I couldn't move. If only people had realised that a muscle relaxant was all I needed. As it was, I was stuck on the sofa at home, unable to do anything. It was a humbling experience, as ever since I was a young child I'd been very independent and never wanted to accept another's help. I didn't realise that I was suffering from pride (which is a sin), but also the 'I don't need anyone' attitude was an irrational belief that had to be broken. I had to leave my front door open so that a stream of people could visit and take care of my needs. It didn't take long to get rid of that particular irrational belief! It was a lesson to me of how my irrational beliefs didn't help me: they hindered me from receiving the very thing that I desired – close relationships with other people.

What if your irrational belief is 'I must never make a mistake'? What happens if you do make one? Does your world come to an end?

Here is a list of some irrational beliefs. Read and tick any that apply to you.

1. 'I am responsible for other people's happiness.'

In place of that irrational belief, take hold of the truth: I am *not* responsible for other people's happiness.

2. 'If people knew me, they wouldn't really like me.'
   This is based on fear and sometimes also on self-rejection or self-hatred. Chapter 10 deals with self-worth and self-esteem.

3. 'I am a failure.'
   We all make mistakes. It's OK to make mistakes; we're not perfect, we don't have to be, because God is.

4. 'I must keep the peace at all costs.'
   Why? Does it make you feel safe?

5. 'If I want something done, I have to do it myself.'
   Why? Don't you trust people?

Take some time out now and think of any other irrational beliefs you may hold.

We can also have in our head negative statements playing from the past like a recording. These are things we've heard said about us over and over – they were enforced in some way.

- 'You're useless – just like your mother/father.'
- 'You're stupid.'
- 'You'll never amount to anything.'
- 'You're unlovable.'
- 'You're not wanted.'
- 'You're a failure.'
- 'It's your fault.'

These things that we have believed about ourselves we need to get rid of, as they're not from God – they're from the enemy. He wants us to believe these things because they hold us and stop us receiving and living in freedom. Usually when Satan says a lie to us, there's a little bit of truth about it – just enough to get us to believe it.

The lie that I used to believe was 'You're stupid'. I believed it and it was a battle for a while, until I realised where it came from. It used to make me defensive in certain situations – I wasn't well educated, so that enforced this lie. Yes, I do make mistakes, but that doesn't make me stupid. This lie went deep, so I still have to keep on my guard to recognise when it's resurfacing.

Sometimes I learn something from the Lord, but then forget, and then I find that the Holy Spirit reminds me again. This next story illustrates my battle and how I can recognise when the enemy is touching my weak spot – that irrational belief that I'm stupid.

A while ago I drove down to our local shops and parked at one end of the village. I did my shopping at both ends of the village and started to walk home. Halfway home, I realised that I had left my car still parked. Into my head came the words, 'You're so stupid, you've left your car parked in the village.' Out loud I said, 'Yes, I know I am. How stupid I am!' Then suddenly I burst out laughing as I realised who was saying this to me. Out loud I then said, 'No, I'm not stupid. I just made a mistake.' Grinning from ear to ear, I retraced my steps to collect my car.

Can you see what happened there? Satan speaks in an accuser's voice: 'You're. . .' If I was having just my own thoughts, however, I would think in the first person: 'I'm. . .' This can be a good way of recognising the accuser's voice. Take time this week to listen to your thought life. How many times do you catch the enemy out speaking to you in this accusing voice? At first you'll find yourself realising after the event, but soon you'll realise as it's happening and can correct it. The Bible says we are to stand against the enemy's schemes, and he will flee.

We're also told in the Bible that Satan is an accuser, a liar and a deceiver, and he masquerades as an angel of light.

Let's pray

Jesus, I realise I have believed things about myself that aren't true. I'm sorry I have believed that. . . (insert what you have believed). *I want to know the truth. Please show me what that is, Jesus. Amen.*

Vows and oaths

Doctors, nurses, judges and solicitors take oaths. These are binding to them. When they're doing their job or living their life, this is their code of practice. As we can see from the following story, oaths and vows can have a profound effect.

I recently read a story about a nun. She had taken her vows of chastity, obedience and poverty, but she had fallen in love and left the order and her convent to get married. After her marriage, her wealthy husband lost his business. After trying for a few years to become pregnant, she realised she was barren. No, she wasn't being punished for leaving the convent and the order: she was still living under the vows and oaths she had taken of chastity and poverty. Someone who was praying for her realised this and asked her to renounce the vows and oaths she had taken years before. The power of those vows was broken and soon afterwards she became pregnant and her husband prospered once more.

When we are threatened, angry or scared, we can make vows or take oaths. We do this using our will and it will continue to have an effect until we choose, with our will, to break that vow, to give it up and renounce it.

To illustrate this, I'll tell you about a girl I met in Holland. This girl – I'll call her Marnie – suffered from depression. She said that friends had told her that she shouted and screamed in her sleep. As I started to pray for her, she felt a pain in her stomach. I asked her if she was remembering anything. She said she was remembering that when she was young her parents were always arguing. I suddenly had a revelation from the Lord that she was sitting on the stairs when this happened. I asked her if this was so, and she said 'yes'. She was recalling this memory clearly, so I asked her to go to the front door in her memory and invite Jesus to come in. Jesus can come back into our yesterdays, as the Bible says he is the same yesterday, today and for ever.

Marnie said that there was a barrier: she wanted to let Jesus in through the front door, but there was something in the way. I asked her if it was dark or light. Often, if there's a barrier stopping someone and it's dark, then it can be some spiritual darkness. She said that yes, it was very dark. Sometimes this spiritual darkness can be there because someone has vowed something, or because they have some sort of belief that has held them. It has the power to be a barrier to receiving freedom.

I explained this and asked Marnie to ask Jesus to show her any vows she may have made. Into her mind came this: that she should be silent and then she wouldn't be blamed for anything she said. This was both a vow and an irrational belief. I also had a revelation of another wrong belief – that she thought she was a bad girl. This would also stop her opening the door to Jesus. Jesus is perfect, and Marnie thought she was bad.

I spoke the words from Scripture where Jesus said, 'Let the little children come to me, and do not hinder them, for the kingdom of heaven belongs to such as these' (Matthew 19:14). Marnie had believed the lie that she was a bad girl. In Jesus' name, I broke the power of that lie and spoke the truth of the scripture over her. As that little girl, she was then able to open the door to Jesus and let him into her memory. She confessed to Jesus her vow of silence, so that she wouldn't get blamed. She renounced it and turned away from it, and in Jesus' name I broke the power of it. She then received the ability to express her emotions, something she couldn't do before. She wasn't silent any more. She cried out her sorrow and her pain, and then allowed Jesus to comfort her.

In Matthew 5:37, Jesus says that the devil is the source of oaths. Oaths can be things such as 'I will never forgive' or 'I will never trust men/women'. When we're hurting, we can make these vows thinking we're protecting ourselves, but they are very strong and binding and need to be dealt with. Until we choose to confess them, ask for forgiveness, turn away from them and break them in Jesus' name, we cannot be free. I've met elderly people who can never cry because they vowed not to cry as a child. This had become such a hindrance to them, as they hadn't had the relief of tears since childhood.

Satan has to have permission from God, Father, Son and Holy Spirit, before doing anything to us. Look up the story of Job in the Old Testament. We also see, in the New Testament, Satan asking Jesus to sift Simon like wheat, to sieve, to test, to accuse and to deceive him. God limits what Satan can do to us. Often we make a choice or make a vow and give the enemy, Satan, an entrance or foothold, and he holds us to it. When we confess our oaths or vows, repent and receive forgiveness, the devil falls away.

Sometimes I've seen people really struggle to choose to renounce a vow they have made. They try to get Jesus to do it for them, but what they need to do is just to choose to do it using their will. I usually say, 'You chose with your will to vow this in the first place, and now you need to choose with your will to reverse it.'

As children, we can make vows out of our distress or fear. A common vow is 'I'm never going to be like my mother/my father'. This is a sad vow, because we often reject traits in us that come from one of our parents. We end up throwing the baby out with the bath water – both their good and their bad traits. I did this with my own mother, who was very creative. I made a vow never to be like her and tried my utmost to be the opposite. It was only years later, after receiving much healing, that I realised I had cut part of myself off – my creative side. Now that I've undone that vow, I've had a release of creativity and spend my leisure time making greetings cards. I'd love to share that with my mother, but unfortunately it's now too late as she has died.

If we're female, we may not celebrate that fact because we made a vow not to be like our mother. We may even hate the gender that we are. Since breaking the vow to do with my own mother, I've also seen that I now not only celebrate my femininity more, but I also embrace it.

If we're male, then maybe our father was academic or cautious and we vowed not to be like him. We may have stunted our own growth in other areas as we tried not to adopt these same traits.

The good news is that it's not too late to change these habits, because it is *for freedom* that Christ has set us free. We're free to choose because we belong to Jesus.

Let's pray. All of the following needs to be said out loud.

Let's pray
Holy Spirit, please come. Jesus, please show me now any vows or oaths I have made regarding my parents or family or myself. Show me any situation where I did this.

Let Jesus bring these things to mind. Think about your parents. What's your relationship like with them? What was it like in the past? Do you think you made a vow about not being like them? Ask Jesus to show you what you vowed. Ask forgiveness for it. Receive his forgiveness.

Now reverse that vow: *In Jesus' name I now choose to break the vow . . .* (name the vow). *I renounce it. I now choose . . .* (choose the opposite to what you vowed – e.g., 'I choose to have a voice', 'I choose to receive everything in me that is like my mother/father', or 'I choose to let people come close').

6: Acknowledging Fear

We seem to like to experience fear – if it means experiencing fear on our own terms, when we know the limits of it. For instance, think of extreme sports or theme park rides, or even people going on television and doing the celebrity jungle thing! We like to take risks under our own terms.

I remember reading a book on child development and learning that three-year-olds use fear as training to be obedient to their parents: they frighten themselves. As I have a three-year-old grandchild, I found this fascinating. I've noticed that recently he talks about monsters and says things like 'That's a bit scary, isn't it?' and asks me if I'm frightened. None of the family has ever spoken about monsters, but his antenna has picked this up. He has also been warned not to put anything small on the floor that will be a danger to his little eight-month-old sister. This has caused him to leap suddenly on anything she touches, shouting out at the top of his voice, '*Danger*!' This probably frightens her so much that she'll be scarred for life! I also realised that we start at an early age to teach children fear when we play peekaboo.

We read about fear being expressed right at the beginning of the Bible in Genesis, when God said to Adam, 'You must not eat from the tree of the knowledge of good and evil.' Then God told him what the *consequence* of doing that would be: 'For when you eat of it you will surely die' (Genesis 2:17). He meant that they were ordained to live for ever, but if Adam ate from this tree there would be no doubt about it: they would definitely die, and they wouldn't be able to change God's mind.

Then Eve was created. I find it interesting that the serpent spoke to Eve, not Adam. He said, 'Did God really say, "You must not eat from any tree in the garden"?' The serpent knew that God hadn't said that – he had only forbidden them to eat from one particular tree. Eve answered, 'We may eat fruit from the trees in the garden, but God did say, "You must not eat fruit from the tree that is in the middle of the garden, and you must not touch it, or you will die." ' This wasn't exactly word for word what God had said to Adam. He didn't say they weren't to touch it, and he said that they would *surely* die. I believe that's why the serpent spoke to Eve. He knew that she wouldn't have taken on board everything that had been said. When we hear something second-hand, we don't usually hear exactly everything that was said, and that's why Eve wasn't precise.

Interestingly, the serpent knew exactly what God had said and he started off his next speech using those exact words: 'You will not surely die . . . For God knows that when you eat of it your eyes will be opened, and you will be like God [that was his hook], knowing good and evil.' We can see here how the serpent started to undermine

LET THE HEALING BEGIN

and challenge what God had said. The way the devil traps us is always through words twisted to sound as if they're a good idea, as if we'll become powerful instead of powerless. He whispers to us, 'You're powerless, but now you can be powerful. . .' The woman Eve looked at the fruit, and it seemed harmless, it looked pleasing to the eye, and the promise of receiving wisdom sounded too good to miss. Just like the serpent, the devil nowadays uses lies and deceit, and he undermines us and what God says to us.

The stages of what happened next, after both Adam and Eve had tasted the fruit of the tree of the knowledge of good and evil, were these:

1. They experienced shame and embarrassment.
2. They stopped relying on God as their provider (they made their own clothes from leaves).
3. They felt guilty about their disobedience.
4. They hid from God in fear.

Also:

5. Death came to some of the animals as God made them clothes from their skins; he provided for them.
6. Pain, suffering and hard work were unleashed upon humankind.
7. They were banished from the garden before they tasted of the tree of life and lived for ever.

All these things happened as a consequence of their sin of taking the fruit.

When people are sinned against, this same pattern of consequences also takes place:

1. We feel shame and embarrassment.

2. We stop trusting and relying on God as provider, and instead provide for ourselves.
3. We feel guilt.
4. We experience fear.

The Bible tells us that the fear of God is the beginning of wisdom (Proverbs 1:7). We are not meant to be afraid of God, but to be *in fear of* God is to be in awe of him, to be aware of how massive, mighty and holy he is. It is an awesome fear. It means knowing that he could strike us down in a second, but that he is also tender, forgiving and merciful. Knowing that he is so much bigger than us is a comfort to us.

Another healthy type of fear is the type that protects us. If we see a fire breaking out, we get frightened, but this means we will protect ourselves and we will minimise our risk of being hurt by fitting smoke detectors and fire alarms and consider where we light candles. An unhealthy fear would be if we break out in a sweat whenever we see someone light a match!

If bad things happened to us when we were young, we could develop a habit of being fearful. We can be scared that we'll be in that position again, so we try to prepare ourselves for the worst. Living in a constant state of fear and anxiety can sometimes lead us on to suffering from phobias.

My own mother was very fearful and anxious and suffered from panic attacks. She also had lots of phobias. Her biggest problem was agoraphobia, a fear of open spaces. She was also frightened of moving water. When she had a bath, it was only in about two or three inches of water.

There was no way she would walk beside a river or any water that moved. She was also on heavy medication, which meant that she couldn't eat cheese and a few other things, otherwise she could have a brain haemorrhage as it would react with the medication. This meant that the fear of eating the wrong things also became a phobia. She cut down her food intake to just a few foods. Every day she ate porridge oats, toast, peaches, chicken, potatoes, runner beans and biscuits. That's all she ate! No other variety in her diet. Then she became fanatical about how the toast was cooked; how the butter was spread; how soft the peaches were. It took over her whole life.

I worked out that her basic fear was the fear of death. We can have lots of fears spurring off that one basic fear: the fear of death. When we have fears and phobias, it means we stop enjoying things, as we fear that things might go wrong.

In 1 Kings 18 we read an interesting story. King Ahab was a wicked man. He'd been looking everywhere for Elijah the prophet, but every time he went to the place where he thought Elijah would be, he'd moved on somewhere else (if only he'd had a mobile phone!). He put his servant Obadiah in charge of his palace. One day Obadiah bumped into Elijah as he was walking along. Instead of being pleased at finding Elijah for his master, Obadiah started projecting forward in his mind, thinking about what he would say when he told his wicked master that he'd found the one he'd been looking for. And then he became afraid that Elijah would disappear before he could get the king to see him. What was Obadiah's fear here? It seems irrational. It was this: if his master the king discovered that once more Elijah had moved on to another district and he couldn't speak with him, he would blame Obadiah and punish him, and it wouldn't be a mild punishment, either. Obadiah said to Elijah, 'You are handing your servant over to be put to death.'

This was the root of Obadiah's fear: the fear of death. As soon as Obadiah saw Elijah, that fear of death came over him as he anticipated what could happen. I've discovered that if we look into our fears and dissect them, they usually come down to just a few basic ones.

The fear that 'I might die' is the fear of death. The fear that 'no one will like me', a fear of rejection, is actually, when we get down to it, a fear of being alone. A fear of intimacy or of letting anyone get close because 'I won't be in control' is actually a fear of not being in control.

In my experience of praying for people over the past 25 years, basic fears usually fall into the following root categories:

1. The fear of death.
2. The fear of being totally alone.
3. The fear of not being in control (being powerless).

I believe that the fear of death started in the Garden of Eden. In the garden the serpent's ploy was to use the words used by God and turn them about. The serpent played on the words 'you will surely die'. We're told in the Bible that sin leads to death. We need to read Romans 8 to understand. But the truth is that up until the time when Jesus walked on the earth, death was in the control of Satan. He had the keys. But Jesus, after his death, descended to hell to get the keys and then ascended to heaven: 'Where, O death, is your sting?' (1 Corinthians 15:55). Satan thought that he had won, that he had sent Jesus to the cross. He didn't realise that it was God the Father's plan to send his Son to die and atone for our sin. Through Jesus we have eternal life, so we will live for ever. We need have no fear of death; we need to proclaim the perfect love of Jesus. Fear loses its power when we dissect it. We give it power by harbouring it.

> God is love. Whoever lives in love lives in God, and God in him. In this way, love is made complete among us so that we will have confidence on the day of judgment, because in this world we are like him. There is no fear in love. But perfect love drives out fear, because fear has to do with punishment. The one who fears is not made perfect in love. (1 John 4:16–18)

This means that if we have fears, we are not whole, because God and fear do not go together. To have one, we have to let go of the other.

Adam and Eve knew fear. They feared punishment, because they had done what God had said they were not to do and they had listened to the serpent that tempted Eve. This fear was a result of sin and the fear made them run away from God. They weren't being punished, they were coming under the consequences of their disobedience.

About ten years ago, I had some symptoms like angina and saw a cardiologist. He told me I had a heart murmur and needed to have an angiogram procedure. He explained I could have a diseased valve and might need an operation, and then quite unemotionally told me that I could have a heart attack during the operation and die. He then casually went on to say that I could even have a heart attack while undergoing the angiogram! He might not have said it in such a cruel way, but that's how it sounded to me.

Without any real facts to help me, I drove home as if I'd just received a death sentence. In my mind I was already dead and buried. My reaction was one of sadness, for my family grieving my death. My sorrow lasted a couple of weeks while I dissected the fear. I came to the conclusion that I couldn't be responsible for my family's feelings if I died, and I needed to have the procedure done to find out the truth of my condition. I also digested the following verse from Scripture:

> Trust in the LORD with all your heart
>   and lean not on your own understanding;
> in all your ways acknowledge him,
>   and he will make your paths straight. (Proverbs 3:5–6)

I didn't just read and meditate on this verse, but I dwelt on it, tasted it and ate it. It became part of me. I dissected each part and emphasised it word by word. It became my lifeline as I chose to live it out. I can honestly say it 'fed' me, just as Jesus said we were to do with God's Word.

After the angiogram procedure, I ended up not having to have an operation and was given some medication. All my initial fears turned out to be unfounded. Saved again!

Fear can consume us so much that we can't think straight. It can hold us in its grip. But if we dissect it, then it loses its power.

> For you did not receive a spirit that makes you a slave again to fear, but you received the Spirit of sonship. And by him [the Holy Spirit] we cry, 'Abba, Father.' (Romans 8:15)

So we see that we're not alone, having received that Spirit

of sonship (male or female, we received it when we became a Christian). We belong to our heavenly Father. Jesus said, 'I will be with you always,' and he meant it. He wasn't lying – he is the truth and he tells the truth.

For instance, let us look at the fear of death. We're all probably a bit scared about the process of dying. It's an unknown quantity. Will it be painful? We don't know. But as Christians we need to know that we have everlasting life. We need have no fear about death. Jesus said that if we know him we will live for ever. The Bible tells us that our body is just a tent. We know that some of us have two-berth ones and some of us have six-berth ones! The part of us that makes up who we really are is the part that will go on to live for ever. Our body will perish, but we will be given another body that will never wear out.

In the Bible it says that fear has to do with punishment. Our fear, then, is that we will be punished. Often we have a wrong view of who God is. Jesus said many times to people, 'Don't be afraid.' He didn't add anything to that, he was simply saying, 'Just don't be. Make a choice not to be.' He knows we get afraid. I've often found it helpful to say out loud, 'I choose not to be afraid; I choose to trust you, Jesus.' But it's definitely a choice we need to make – it doesn't just happen.

> When I am afraid,
>> I will trust in you.
> In God, whose word I praise,
>> in God I trust; I will not be afraid.
>> What can mortal man do to me? (Psalm 56:3–4)

Are we going to choose to believe Jesus and his promises, or Satan and his lies?

Let's pray

Let's ask the Holy Spirit to come and show us if we have a fear of death. Ask him to surface anything from the past that was the root of that. (You may find it helpful to have someone else there to pray with you.) Renounce the fear of death and open yourself up to receive life in all its fullness in Jesus' name. Use some of the scriptures at the end of this chapter to pray through.

I used to have a fear that gripped me whenever I was in an aeroplane, usually halfway through the journey. I asked someone at my church to pray for me. As they prayed, I remembered death had come close to me twice, once as I was born and once when I was two. My friend broke the power of the fear of death over me and I experienced something lifting off me, leaving what felt like a space inside me. I haven't had this fear gripping me since.

How about the next root fear, the fear of being alone? Sometimes this can go back to childhood, when something bad happened and the feelings of anger, pain or grief were not released. Often when I've prayed with someone and asked Jesus to surface any memories he wants to heal, that person remembers being alone in a room and feeling totally alone and abandoned. I ask them to stand up in that memory, to go and open the door and let Jesus come in to be with them, as he is the same yesterday, today and for ever and wants to come and visit our yesterdays.

The serpent in the Garden of Eden tried to get between Adam and Eve by going to speak to Eve alone, in order to undermine their relationship so that the trust was broken between them. When trust is broken, it alienates us and makes us feel lonely.

Jesus said, 'I am with you always, to the very end of the age' (Matthew 28:20). It's a forever love. We're often fed lies by the enemy, Satan – lies such as 'You'll be alone', 'You won't have anyone', and so on.

It's our fear that makes us a slave, and it's our attitude of fear that stops people getting close to us. We can give off negative vibes: 'You wouldn't want to know me if you knew that. . .' Then we try too hard to make friends, and that's the thing that puts people off and stops them getting close. This then fulfils our fear that we won't have any friends and that we'll be all alone.

The Bible speaks of fear seizing or gripping someone, or of them trembling with fear. Fear can make us incapable of action. We need to recognise fears from the past that affect us now – those that grip us and prevent us from action.

In the Bible we're told the story of the talents. One person was given the equivalent of £1,000, one was given £2,000, another was given £4,000. Two of the people put their money to work and invested it, and it made more money. The person who had been given £1,000 did nothing with it and buried it instead. He was afraid that he might do the wrong thing and waste it. I believe he was filled with the fear of rejection. He misunderstood what his master was like. He had a fear of failure and didn't use the money or invest it. He probably also feared that he would be compared to the others if they were more successful. His fear actually stopped him from doing the right thing. I think that if we dissected those fears, we would see at the root of them the fear of being all alone. If he was rejected or not as good as others – a failure – then he might be left all alone.

We may inherit fear from a parent, and then end up copying what we experience around us.

After the tragedy of our daughter's death, I started to get panicky in crowds. I asked the Holy Spirit to show me why I did this. He refreshed my memory of my mother taking me to the shops when I was really young. She was frightened of being outside due to her agoraphobia; she kept clasping and unclasping my hand, her own hands dripping with sweat. Then I identified where the fear had come from, so I prayed actively every day about it. In Jesus' name, I cut myself off from my mother's fear of crowds and open spaces. I asked Jesus to take anything that I had learned from my mother through her fear and asked him to deliver me from anything that she had passed on to me. Within a week I had lost my sense of panic in crowds.

Other things in our family life can also affect us and make us fearful:

- Superstition in the family: 'Don't do . . . or something bad will happen to you.'
- Unpredictable home life: 'What will I find when I get home today?'

This is what the LORD says. . .
'Fear not, for I have . . . summoned you by name.' (Isaiah 43:1)

Another fearful time I remember is when I stayed in a

stranger's house. I'd been involved in preparing the first New Wine festival, so I was already feeling exhausted, but staying in a stranger's house also had an effect on my feelings of insecurity. The house was very big and old, and I found it difficult to get any bearings, especially in the middle of the night! I needed to go to the toilet, so I made my way to the bathroom and, not wanting to wake the other guests, I decided not to put the light on. This was a huge mistake. As I came out of my room, I felt my way along the corridor. It was pitch black. I managed to make my way to the bathroom without a hitch. Unfortunately my problems started when I left the bathroom and switched off the light as I stepped out onto the landing. Suddenly I was plunged into the blackest darkness I'd ever experienced. I stood still and waited for my night eyes to kick in, but it didn't happen. Then fear started to grip me. I strained my eyes, but still I could see nothing. Next I started crawling along the floor, my arms waving about frantically as I tried to feel something, anything that would give me a sense of perspective and direction. Panic was about to set in, and I could feel I was on the verge of screaming uncontrollably, but as I crawled along bit by bit, I eventually felt the banister of the stairs. Phew! What a relief.

Recapping on that story, what do you think my fear was in this instance? I feared what I couldn't see! I wasn't in control of the situation, so I couldn't be prepared for what might happen. Often this is our fear in everyday life. It can then get completely out of proportion and we can put in place safeguards so that we'll never be out of control. We can become controlling, not just of our own lives, but of those around us. All our reason just flies out of the window. We can then get stuck with habitual behaviour.

This third root fear is so common. We probably all want to be in control to some extent, but we need to give control of our lives over to Jesus. When we first became a Christian, it may be that we asked Jesus into our life but never went to the next stage of actually surrendering our life to Jesus, giving over the control to him. We may have had times in the past when others were powerful, causing us to feel utterly powerless. God is our hiding place; he is the one to run to. Remember that the serpent used this same thing, tempting Eve to become powerful.

Do you remember ever having those feelings of fear? Your legs feel as if they've turned to jelly, your heart is pounding, or else your whole body becomes alert for sudden action. Your blood starts to pump faster and it feels as if your ears are out on stalks and every nerve of your body is taut, ready for action.

Our bodies were made to react and respond to fear. To us fear signals danger. Our body gets ready for it and becomes completely alert. It gets ready for one of two things, either to run away from danger, or to stand up and fight. It's known as the 'fight or flight' response. This is a basic, automatic response. Sometimes we can get into this 'fight or flight' response as an everyday way of life. Maybe a frightening experience sparked it off, and this set up a recurring reaction. Maybe every time we see something vaguely out of the ordinary, we may respond in this way – either by running away or by wanting to fight. After a while we can develop an anxiety that's there most of the time.

Have you heard of that saying, 'The best form of defence is attack'? We can get into a habit of verbally attacking people because deep down we're scared and fearful. Or maybe we avoid confrontation because we want to run away – we may perceive that danger is lurking. We need to discover what the things are that we fear, so that we can find out what the basis of our fear is.

Let's pray
Jesus, please come now by the power of the Holy Spirit and show me some of my fears. Open me up, Lord, to memories of the past. Show me any fear that gripped me then and still does now. I give you permission to go into those closed-off places in my memories. Amen.

Here is a list of some common fears. Ask the Holy Spirit to show you which ones you have and ask him to work through them. Tell him that you're willing to face them and look at them so that they will lose the power to hold you.

We all have fears, big or small. Add to the list any other fears that the Holy Spirit is bringing to mind.

- Fear of Satan
- Fear of death
- Fear of authority
- Fear of failure
- Fear of not being loved . . . by God, by others
- Fear of not being able to love others
- Fear of intimacy

- Fear of marriage
- Fear of never getting married
- Fear of being alone
- Fear of the dark
- Fear of divorce
- Fear of never having children
- Fear of having children
- Fear of rejection
- Fear of disapproval
- Fear of confrontation
- Fear of being broke
- Fear of the future
- Fear of not being in control
- Fear of death of a loved one
- Fear of mental illness
- Fear of being or becoming homosexual
- Fear of being a victim of crime
- Fear of specific people, animals, objects
- Fear of being left alone
- Fear of God
- List any others

When you've worked your way down the list, try to follow the action points set out below.

1. Have a look at your list. Are any of the fears you have ticked connected with one another?
2. Look at each fear in turn. When did this fear first start? Was it an event in the past?
3. Look at these fears and see which of them are based on lies.
4. Realise that your fears have prevented you from living

a victorious life. Confess to Jesus what those fears are, receive forgiveness and choose to believe the truth.

5. Then look at these fears and dissect them to see them in the light of the three basic fears: fear of death, fear of being alone, and fear of loss of control.

Let's pray

Father, I realise I have fears from the past that affect me today. Please reveal what those fears are. I want to dissect them, to expose them and work through them. I don't want to live under this fear any more. I want to be filled with your perfect love that casts out fear. Fill me with you now, Lord. Banish the fear of . . . (name the fear). *I choose to let go now of the fear of . . .* (name the fear) *in Jesus' name, and I now choose to live in the security of your love for me. In Jesus' name. Amen.*

Fear can make us want to avoid situations like confrontation, and we put into place a coping mechanism so that we can avoid what we fear. Fear of not being accepted, for example, can make us a 'people-pleaser' or a 'clown'.

Years ago I was so scared that people would laugh at me. One of my fears was that I would trip over when I crossed a room and everyone would laugh at me. I was so afraid that I would look or sound like a fool. This meant that I did things to make people laugh so that I was in control of when they laughed. I would rather they laughed with me than at me. What was my fear here? It was that no one would like me, and the root of that fear was that I was afraid I'd be all alone.

Many of us use other types of survival strategies, such as

rescuing people but getting burned out in the process of wanting to be needed. Or we can be totally dependent on someone, clinging to them so much that we nearly suffocate them. Or we can become an attention seeker. We can choose always to be in control, never delegating, never putting ourselves in a vulnerable position. Another coping strategy is to be aggressive and hostile, protecting ourselves, keeping others at arms' length emotionally. Or else we can be totally independent almost to the point of rudeness, hiding our emotions and making our own world of safety. We can be demanding of attention, easily grieved, an exhibitionist, or a drama king or queen. Or we can act out being the victim as our identity, wearing it like a garment. Rather than face the hard things in life, we can also become addicted to one of the following: sex, shopping, work, worry, food, drugs or sport, doing all sorts of things other than facing the fear, insecurity and pain.

Let's pray

*Father, I realise I've used coping strategies. Show me what they are, because I want to change. I want to live a life of freedom under your protection. Please show me where I've become addicted to things that just cover up the pain and fear. Show me what they are now. (*Take time for the Holy Spirit to show you. Say out loud those things that you've identified.) *I renounce these ways now. Jesus, please free me from them. Where they have bound me, loose them, Jesus. I choose now to give these ways of coping up to you. From this moment I choose a life of liberty and freedom in your name. Amen.*

I fear that my greatest fear will come upon me! Have you heard that one? We can often speak negatively to ourselves without even realising it. Have you ever said any of the following?

- 'I'm getting a cold.'
- 'My legs/back/arms are killing me.'
- 'My back will be the death of me.'
- 'I bet I'm ill when I go on holiday.'

Do you get my drift? So often we live our lives in a negative way, full of fear. Why don't we live in hope? We know Jesus – he is our living hope. He is the author and perfecter of our faith. Like it says in the Bible, let us throw off everything that doesn't belong.

Let's pray

Father, I confess that I've got into negative habits of thought. Please forgive me. Please break the cycle of thought patterns that are negative and destructive. I want to live in freedom. Please renew my mind by the power of your Holy Spirit. Amen.

Our unresolved fear can also cause phobias. I told you earlier of a few phobias my mother had. It was good to see that when she became a Christian at the age of 62, she was baptised and fully immersed in water without any fear – amazing, considering that she only ever bathed in two inches of water!

After an accident during childhood when I fell through a cold frame in the garden and deeply cut my leg through to the bone, I had a phobia about broken glass. Whenever I saw broken glass, I came out in a sweat and felt really hot, dizzy and nauseous. This went on for many years, until one day before I got engaged Ken said to me, 'We can tackle this together. Let me help you.' It felt really scary, but I agreed. One day there was some broken glass at my feet and usually I would get someone else to clear it up. This time Ken took hold of the dustpan and brush and put them into my hands. Then he put his own hands over the top of mine and said, 'Come on, we can do this together. There's no need to be afraid.' Shaking with fear, I allowed him to guide me towards the broken glass. He kept up a continual flow of encouragement as we swept the glass into the dustpan. At the end I needed to sit down for a while, but he praised me for my effort. Over the next few months he must either have sought out broken glass, or deliberately broken it himself! Many times together we cleared up the glass with his hands on top of mine, until one day I was able to do it alone. Thinking about it now, it sounds foolish, but to me it was a very real fear. I was so pleased that Ken helped me by desensitising me to this object fear.

Another big fear I had was of swimming out of my depth (I mentioned this in Chapter 1). Regularly I had dreams about it and woke in a sweat with my heart pounding. When I was growing up, no one in my immediate family could swim. I learned aged 30 when I was pregnant. My hope was that the increase in my size would make me more buoyant! At that time we were involved in open youth work with some young people who hung out on the streets every night. I met a young girl aged 14 called Amy. She'd just passed her gold medal lifesaving exam. As we were talking, I explained my fear of swimming out of my depth. Amy said that she wanted to help me, so we arranged to meet at the local swimming pool the following week.

My nervousness was really showing as we entered the swimming pool. Round and round in my head went the thought, 'I can't believe at my age that I'm going to trust a 14-year-old with my life!' The only thing that gave me courage was to keep thinking that I wanted to conquer this fear so that I wouldn't keep having nightmares about it, plus the fact that I didn't want to look a fool in front of her and lose my street cred! Amy swam by my side down the centre of the whole length of the pool and back. All the while she was encouraging me, saying, 'Well done, I'm not going to let anything happen to you, and if it does I'm able to save you.' God used this young girl to disperse my fear. I was so proud of her and of myself after I'd done it, and from then on I never had another dream of drowning or swimming out of my depth. Once more fear lost its power as it was looked full in the face!

We need to look at the truth in the Bible. Is it true? It's either the truth or a lie. If we say it's the truth, then we need to believe it and live with that truth inside us instead of the fear.

Right now, choose not to be afraid. Out loud say, 'In Jesus' name I choose not to be afraid.'

Read the following scriptures and then use them to pray, to receive and to live out of this truth:

> The LORD is my light and my salvation –
>   whom shall I fear?

> The LORD is the stronghold of my life –
>   of whom shall I be afraid? (Psalm 27:1)

So do not fear, for I am with you;
 do not be dismayed, for I am your God.
I will strengthen you and help you;
 I will uphold you with my righteous right hand.
All who rage against you
 will surely be ashamed and disgraced. . .
For I am the LORD, your God,
 who takes hold of your right hand
and says to you, Do not fear;
 I will help you. (Isaiah 41:10–13)

Here are some promises of Jesus:

I will never leave you nor forsake you.
Fear not, for I am with you.
I am with you always.
Do not worry about anything.
Do not be afraid.
I no longer call you servants; you are my friends.

For we know that since Christ was raised from the dead, he cannot die again; death no longer has mastery over him. (Romans 6:9)

My grace is sufficient for you. (2 Corinthians 12:9)

There is no fear in love. But perfect love drives out fear, because fear has to do with punishment. The one who fears is not made perfect in love. (1 John 4:18)

The LORD is with me; I will not be afraid.
 What can man do to me? (Psalm 118:6)

But as for me, it is good to be near God.
 I have made the Sovereign LORD my refuge;
 I must tell of all your deeds. (Psalm 73:28)

Come near to God and he will come near to you. (James 4:8)

. . . the very hairs of your head are all numbered. So don't be

LET THE HEALING BEGIN

afraid; you are worth more than many sparrows. (Matthew 10:30–31)

He will wipe every tear from their eyes. There will be no more death or mourning or crying or pain, for the old order of things has passed away. (Revelation 21:4)

When you pass through the waters,
    I will be with you;
and when you pass through the rivers,
    they will not sweep over you. . . . (Isaiah 43:2)

Having disarmed the powers and authorities, he made a public spectacle of them, triumphing over them by the cross. (Colossians 2:15)

For God so loved the world that he gave his one and only Son, that whoever believes in him shall not perish but have eternal life. (John 3:16)

Also read the whole of Psalms 91, 139 and 23.

7: Releasing and Receiving Forgiveness

Have you got a dog, or do you know someone who has one? They're the most forgiving creatures. Our dog was called Gemma and she lived to the grand age of 15, which in human years equals 105! Gemma never bore a grudge and never kept a record of wrongs. I'm sure that our Creator gave us the animals to teach us things, and dogs definitely show us a little bit about the subject of forgiveness.

If I ever trod on Gemma's paw, she would yelp with pain, but immediately, before I could even get the word 'sorry' out of my mouth, she would lick my hand as if to say, 'It's OK, I forgive you.' She had no hesitation, and immediately our relationship was restored. Don't you wish it was like that with all of our relationships? No one else has ever responded to me in the way Gemma did (not that I'd want anyone else to lick me!).

When I went away for a few days, or even if I left her

with someone for a week or two, on my return she'd be the first one to greet me at the door. Her tail would be wagging a greeting. No guilt trip was put on me for leaving her; she would just show her immense pleasure at seeing me with no blame for my absence. She would always be affectionate, and if she was sitting close to me she would even lick my bare feet!

If she ever did anything wrong (which was rare), my response would be nothing like hers. She rarely peed on the carpet (only if she was ill), but if she did I would immediately shoo her out of the back door and as a punishment would keep her out there for a while. It would make me angry, and it would take me a while to forgive her.

Even at the end of her life, as she was being held before having the lethal drug injected into her by the vet, she looked at me with eyes of love, saying, 'It's OK. I understand.'

Cats seem to react in a very different way. They *do* bear a grudge. If we ever went away and left our cat (during our married life we must have had at least six cats), arranging for someone else to come in and feed it, the cat would punish us when we arrived home. Our cat would sit nearby, but not too close, with its back to us to show us its displeasure. This would continue throughout our first day back at home. Although we're nothing like our pets, in some ways they show us many traits that can be examples to adopt or to shun.

One Easter, when I was about twelve, I remember saying to my mum as I bit into my hot cross bun, 'What's the point of the cross on the bun? What does it mean? Why is Good Friday called Good Friday? What was the point of

Jesus dying on a cross? It seems a bit silly to me!' To each of my questions, she said that she didn't know the answer.

Do *we* really know? Will we ever know the fullness of what Jesus did on the cross for us? Many people have tried to explain it, both in simple ways and in intellectual ways, sometimes using diagrams or drama. So many people have tried to explain it, but there's no better place than the Bible to show us the answer to our questions.

In 1 Corinthians 1:18, we read, 'For the message of the cross is foolishness to those who are perishing, but to us who are being saved it is the power of God.' In the Living Bible translation, this passage (vv. 18–31) reads:

> I know very well how foolish it sounds to those who are lost when they hear that Jesus died to save them. But we who are saved recognise this message as the very power of God. For God says, 'I will destroy all human plans of salvation no matter how wise they seem to be, and ignore the best ideas of men, even the most brilliant of them.'
>
> So what about these wise men, these scholars, these brilliant debaters of this world's great affairs? God has made them all look foolish, and shown their wisdom to be useless nonsense. For God in his wisdom saw to it that the world would never find God through human brilliance, and then he stepped in and saved all those who believed his message, which the world calls foolish and silly. It seems foolish to the Jews because they want a sign from heaven as proof that what is preached is true; and it is foolish to the Gentiles because they believe only what agrees with their philosophy and seems wise to them. So when we preach about Christ dying to save them, the Jews are offended and the Gentiles say it is all nonsense. But God has opened the eyes of those called to salvation, both Jews and Gentiles, to see that Christ is the mighty power of God to save them; Christ himself is the cen-

tre of God's wise plan for their salvation. This so called 'foolish' plan of God is far wiser than the wisest plan of the wisest man, and God in his weakness – Christ dying on the cross – is far stronger than any man.

Notice among yourselves, dear brothers, that few of you who follow Christ have big names or power or wealth. Instead, God has deliberately chosen to use ideas of the world considered foolish and of little worth to shame those people considered by the world as wise and great. He has chosen a plan despised by the world, counted as nothing at all, and used it to bring down to nothing those the world considers great, so that no one anywhere can ever boast in the presence of God.

For it is from God alone that you have your life through Christ Jesus. He showed us God's plan of salvation; he was the one who made us acceptable to God; he made us pure and holy and gave himself to purchase our salvation. As it says in the scriptures, 'If anyone is going to boast, let him boast only of what the Lord has done.'

On the television soap *Eastenders*, in the days when it was entertaining, there was an episode that was very moving. One of the characters, Dot, an elderly Bible-bashing Christian who actually caused Christians to cringe, was mugged in her own home, beaten up and landed in hospital. When she came out a few weeks later she was bitter and hurt and had lost her faith. She said that God hadn't saved her from the robbery and mugging. Feeling let down, she changed personality, which worried her non-Christian husband. Dot wouldn't go to church, read her Bible or spout scriptures to everyone in earshot like she usually did. Then she had to go and identify the mugger in a line-up at the police station.

As she looked at the young man in his late teens in the line-up, she realised that she didn't hate him. In fact, she had pity on him – he was young and foolish; he was some-one's son. Dot realised that she had forgiven him. Then Dot was shown in her church on her own, speaking to Jesus while she looked at a figure representing him on the cross. She said, 'I know you're real because I don't hate any more. I couldn't have done what I just did, I couldn't have forgiven him.' Dot realised that she was forgiven and Jesus had enabled her to forgive that young man. Then Jim, her husband, walked into the church behind her. He looked up at the cross and said, 'Thank you, Jesus, for giving Dot back to me.'

Although it was only a story in a television soap, I cried. I cried because it was the truth. Jesus does forgive and that's how we can forgive others, and yes, people are restored to us and we are restored to them. Reconciliation and restoration can follow forgiveness.

Jesus forgives and restores us and asks us to pass on what he freely gives to us. When we hate people who have hurt us, we sin. No matter what they have done to us and however bad it was, we sin when we harbour bitterness, anger or hatred. Jesus wants to forgive us our sin, and then he asks us to pass on the forgiveness we have received to those who have sinned against us. By doing this, we're not saying that what that person did was OK; we're choos-ing not to let that poison affect us any more.

When someone hurts us badly, we say things like, 'I'll never forget that' – and the truth is, we don't! We say, 'I'll never forgive him/her for doing that to me' – and we don't. We like keeping a record of wrongs.

I told you a bit about my relationship with my mum. I'd forgiven her for letting me down, but deep down I still had a lot of unforgiveness towards her. To my dismay, I started hearing repeated stories of people telling one of their parents that they loved them. One day it was on the radio, another day on the television. I even started reading stories about this in magazines or in the newspaper. This went on for about three months. The impression that I should do the same thing for my mother first of all started as a whisper, but seemed to be growing into something like a shout! All this time I was arguing with the Lord, saying, 'There's no way that I'm going to tell my mum I love her, because the fact is, I *don't*! And even if I did, I'm almost 40 years old, far too old to be saying such a thing!'

Eventually, while I was taking communion one Sunday, I said to the Lord, 'OK, I don't actually love her, but if you give me your love for her, I'll tell her – but it's up to you, not me, because I can't tell her something that's a lie.'

My mum and dad had been visiting for the weekend, and I went home from church realising that it was time to take them to the station for their journey home. I was still battling with the Holy Spirit when we set off. We arrived at the station, and as we got out of the car I heard an inner voice say to me, 'Now, say it now.'

I stood close to my mum and said, 'I know you'll never believe this, but I do love you.' As I said those words, the most incredible love surged through my entire body. This wasn't the love of Jesus for my mum – it was *my* love, the love that I thought had been eaten away. This was the love of a child for her mum.

My mum burst into tears and said, 'I've so wanted to hear that! I was saying to your aunty the other day that I so wished you would say that to me.'

By this point I too was sobbing, and then, to my utter surprise and shock, out of my mouth came some words that bypassed my brain: 'But what about me? Why have *you* never told *me* that you loved *me*?' It was like the cry of the inner child. The strangest thing was that I didn't *know* that my mum had never uttered those words to me, but obviously the Lord knew that I needed to ask her this. He knew what we both needed.

She replied, 'Of course I love you. I don't know why I could never say it when you were little.' Then (and this next bit is a bit embarrassing) she said, 'I love you. You will always be my baby.' We sobbed into each other's arms, mother and daughter reconciled as healing took place.

I'm not going to lie and say that from then on our relationship was perfect, far from it, but there was a huge difference. When I telephoned her, I no longer held the telephone away from my ear, giving occasional grunts – I actually listened to her. When she told me about her ailments and her struggle with depression, I felt compassion for her. The love that had been unleashed stayed with me even though she frustrated the life out of me at times. Deep down I knew that she loved me and that I loved her, and that made all the difference. In fact, towards the end of her life I rang her three times a day, because she was in need of mental and emotional assurance.

It cost me a lot to say those words 'I love you', but what I did was nothing compared to what it cost Jesus to say 'I love you' to us. Jesus showed us that forgiveness was costly; it cost God our Father his Son. Forgiveness goes against all our ideas of justice, which usually demands a payment for the wrongs we have suffered. Jesus forgives us

LET THE HEALING BEGIN

at a great cost to himself and asks for no repayment from us. He just asks that we do the same. Forgiveness is costly, and so is love. We'll never fully understand what an amazing sacrifice Jesus made. None of us could come anywhere close to matching it. But what we can do is receive it and pass it on to others.

Read the story of Joseph in the Old Testament to refresh your memory. Let God show you forgiveness as shown by Joseph. What torture he must have suffered all those years in prison. He worked through it until he could forgive his relatives and also bless them.

On a television programme scientists were showing experiments aimed at finding out the worst smells, as they wanted to find an ultimate smell to be used as a weapon against people who were rioting. Guess what the worst smells were? The worst ones they discovered were vomit, excrement and rotting animal flesh. They then asked some people to go into various cubicles, and they blew this smell via tubes directly into people's nostrils. Almost immediately, one guy pulled off the electrodes and pulled out the tubes in his nostrils and ran away from that cubicle as fast as his legs would take him. He was retching from the disgusting smell.

This is a little illustration of what our sin smells like to God. It stinks. It is a stench in his nostrils. Is that shocking to you? Sometimes we need to get graphic to understand what our sin is really like to God. Sometimes we need to be shocked into realising what our sin is like to God.

Do you remember, from when you last vomited, what it looked like, what it tasted and smelled like? When Jesus went on the cross, it was as if in his purity and holiness he put his body on our vomit of sin and soaked it up, as if his body was a sponge-like garment. That sounds as if I'm reducing Jesus to a garment, but I'm just trying to help you see how awful our sin is and what a wonderful thing Jesus did when he took it upon himself. We will not fully know until we get to heaven what it cost Jesus to die for us. The Bible tells us that now we only see as if 'through a glass darkly' – it isn't clear. We can't begin to forgive people who have hurt us in the past if we haven't any idea what *our* sin is like and what Jesus did on the cross for us. God doesn't forgive excuses, he forgives sin.

We need to see this as a revelation, to confess our sin of bitterness, fear, anger, rage, hatred, revenge, fear, guilt, shame and rejection, and to receive, truly receive, the forgiveness that is offered to us.

A while ago, when our little grandchild Ted was three months old, he hadn't done a poo for seven days. He was a breastfed baby, so normally he would be expected to have a bowel movement after every feed. So you can imagine that seven days' worth was not very good for a little baby; it made him very uncomfortable. The health visitor suggested putting him in the bath and holding him in a sitting position whilst gently massaging his lower tummy. His mum and dad were both holding and helping Ted in the bath. After a little while, the floodgates opened and Ted started pushing out all this stuff that had impacted in his tummy. He cried in his distress as he pushed out all this poo. There was so much of it that it went all over his mum's and dad's arms. In fact, he went on pooing for at least 20 minutes! All the while, his mum and dad were looking into his eyes and saying, 'We love you, Ted!'

That's what Jesus does for us. He looks into our eyes as we let out our stink of sin all over him, and he says, 'I love you.'

He said 'I love you' as he was nailed on the cross, and he says it now. It took longer than 20 minutes – it was the whole sin of the whole world, all we've ever done and all we'll ever do. He who knew no sin became a sin offering once and for all, so that we could come to him without shame.

In the Bible it says that when we were far off, before we ever knew anything about God, *he knew us*. He knew all the sin we would ever commit, but he loved us anyway. The cross was symbolic of torture; it was known as a curse to be crucified, and Jesus became that curse. God is holy and under the old covenant blood had to be shed by the sacrifice of an animal and the priest would proclaim atonement for sins so that they could be forgiven. Jesus the Lamb of God became that sacrifice, that offering, because the sin and depravity had become so bad in the world that the usual sacrifices would no longer do. It had to be something pure, clean and holy. There wasn't anything in the world like that, so God had to come to earth himself. He sent his son Jesus Christ, who left everything in heaven and came to earth as a vulnerable baby so that we wouldn't be frightened of him, so that we could identify with him. He relied totally on his Father and on the Holy Spirit. Jesus wanted to show us what his – and our – heavenly Father is like. He wanted to show us that he identifies with us in our pain and suffering.

He suffered physical abuse over and over; he was hounded from place to place, betrayed by his friends, lied to, rejected, despised, abandoned and mocked; he had nowhere of his own to sleep. He was misunderstood many times and his actions were questioned. At the worst time of his torture he said, 'Father, forgive them, for they do not know what they are doing' (Luke 23:34).

Will you come to the cross today as a symbol of receiving what he did for you? Will you receive this wonderful forgiveness? Will you come and lay down your pain and choose to forgive?

Forgiveness opens up the way for healing to take place. We need to let go of the blame and start working through some of our issues. That doesn't mean that what was done to us was OK and acceptable. It means that we're choosing not to hold on to it any more: we're not going to allow this poison to permeate our body, mind and spirit any more. We can't offer to others what we don't have ourselves. We need now to come to the cross and receive the forgiveness that is freely offered. Only then can we offer it to those who need it. This isn't going to be easy, but it is necessary. We're all sinners, and total forgiveness isn't a feeling, it's an act. None of us deserves it, but it's an act of the will – we choose to do it.

At first it has nothing to do with feelings, but later on, when we have totally forgiven someone, we do have feelings. It feels good to forgive. How do we know when we have totally forgiven someone? When it doesn't hurt any more. We may have to forgive over and over and let go of the pain bit by bit. But each time it gets a little easier. Sometimes it feels as if you're taking one step forward and two steps back, but keep pressing on with it. Every time it hurts, wherever you are and whatever you're doing,

LET THE HEALING BEGIN

choose with your mind to forgive and bring that person to the cross in your mind and release forgiveness to them.

Forgiveness is a huge act; it's spiritual and dynamic. We don't understand it, but it has the power in the spiritual realm to change things. It must be one of the most powerful things, because Jesus would not have chosen this way otherwise.

Forgiveness is a command, not an option. As Jesus says in the Bible, 'Forgive, and you will be forgiven' (Luke 6:37).

Sometimes we realise that we're holding things against God. We may think that we need to forgive God. He is perfect, so he doesn't need forgiving as he hasn't done anything wrong, but what needs to happen is for us to lay down our blame, where we've blamed God for the evil that has been done to us. We need to choose with our mind to let that go. This is a massive barrier when it comes to us being able to receive all that God is offering to us. We're not going to receive good things from someone against whom we've erected a barrier.

Sometimes we need to forgive ourselves, to stop blaming ourselves for what happened. There was an article in the *Daily Express* a couple of years ago by a psychologist from a university, saying that there was a strong link between our emotions and our immune system, and he listed ten points that could lead to freedom.

1. Stop excusing, pardoning or rationalising.
2. Pinpoint the actions that have hurt you.
3. Spend time thinking of ways in which your life would be more satisfying if you could let go of your grievances.

4. Try replacing angry thoughts about the 'badness' of the perpetrator with thoughts about how the offender is also a human being who is vulnerable to harm.

5. Identify yourself with the offender's probable state of mind. Understand the perpetrator's history, while not condoning his or her actions.

6. Spend some time developing greater compassion towards the perpetrator.

7. Become more aware that you have needed others' forgiveness in the past.

8. Make a heartfelt resolution not to pass on your own pain to others.

9. Enjoy the sense of emotional relief that comes when the burden of grudge has melted away. Enjoy also the feeling of goodwill and mercy you have shown.

10. Spend time appreciating the sense of purpose and direction that comes after steps 1 to 8.

This was all in a secular context. How much more as Christians are we commanded to forgive.

Yes, Jesus will help us, but we have to make a move with our will. For some of us, it will start with just wanting to want to forgive. We have to start somewhere, so if this is you, it's better to start than to refuse. I want to tell you now of a personal story.

One of the things that I found difficult to forgive and that still affects me in some ways, especially in the area of trusting people, has to do with the birth of our first child, Sarah. She was stillborn, with the deformity of a tiny brain.

When I was in labour and first went into hospital, all

the doctors and nurses told me was that they needed to get the baby out early and that she would be premature by about four weeks. They said they would be able to treat her outside the womb to give her the things she needed for her development.

The doctors and nurses told me everything was going to be fine. They even put a little baby cot in the room with me. They even told me what they would do when she was born.

Unknown to me, they could see on the X-ray they took that she would be born dead. They knew that what they were telling me was all lies. They even told Ken and told him not to tell me. My poor husband had to watch me for two days and nights during a very painful labour and listen to me telling him how wonderful it would be when our baby was born. It must have been tearing him apart. Then they did something really bad. The midwife let two student nurses practise on me. They examined me internally many times during those two days. The pain was excruciating. They were very young and seemed to have no care about what they were doing to me, but chatted amongst themselves instead. They caused me so much stress and pain that was really unnecessary.

Eventually I gave birth. At this point they threw a sheet over our newly born baby and the doctor said, 'I'm sorry, Mrs Morgan, your baby is dead.' The room had been full of people, but suddenly they all left. They left me screaming, with Ken trying to comfort me. There was no sign of our baby. They never showed me my baby, or even told me what they did with her. To this day I have no idea where she is buried. We weren't given any options for her burial, as in those days people didn't realise that it was important. She was discarded as an ugly object, like a piece of rubbish.

After the birth I was put into a ward full of mothers with their babies. They put me in a room with windows all around it and shut the curtains as if I was an embarrassment to everyone. I felt like the object of everyone's pity, and they looked through the door with expressions of guilt. During the night the cries of the babies kept me awake, but also pierced me with the thought that I wanted a baby that could cry. I only stayed in the hospital for one night, but the damage had been done.

Not only had many people repeatedly lied to me, but they had made my husband lie to me and they didn't show me my baby. No one ever showed that they cared. I'm sure now that they must have cared, but they'd been taught not to show emotions in front of the patients.

I felt as if I was an embarrassment to everyone, and was filled with guilt that I had somehow killed my own baby. Very occasionally it still hurts a bit. We had a daughter we'd never seen. For seven years I was so repulsed by thoughts of what she must have looked like, because no one had ever bothered to explain the condition to me. My imagination produced images far more horrific than anything they could have shown to me. Eventually, years later, I went to a library and looked up anencephaly babies in a medical textbook. It wasn't half as awful as I'd imagined. About ten years later, I had a dream and Jesus showed me what she looks like now. I met her in my dreams!

I don't tell you this to make you feel sorry for us – it was a long time ago – but I wanted to show you that I know that forgiving people isn't easy, that it can be painful. We can so easily justify what people do to us and make excuses for them, or try to find a reason for what they did so that it might be easier to cope with, but the fact remains that the only way to be free of pain is to forgive totally.

When we get hurt and don't forgive, we become a victim of the other person and feel justified in living in self-pity and victimhood. By shifting the blame and making excuses for our own behaviour or responses, we never allow God to search our hearts about our own issues. After we forgive, we have to ask Jesus to bless those who have hurt us. This too is painful, but it leads to reconciliation.

I don't hold myself up as an example. I hold Jesus up as the example, because he alone has the power to forgive. He is the restoring one and he calls us into restoration with himself and with other relationships. In some cases of abuse, however, this is not possible. For some people this could be dangerous and unwise. Wherever possible, ask Jesus how this can happen in a practical way.

Make the following your prayer, using your own words if you prefer. Make it heartfelt, and make it personal and meaningful.

Let's pray
Please come, Holy Spirit. Jesus, I welcome you with your passion and compassion. Come to me now with the power of the cross. Please come with the power of forgiveness. I want to receive it and give it away. I confess to you any resentment and unforgiveness I have. Please show to me what I have inside that needs confessing to you.

Now ask for forgiveness, and receive it.

Please show me now, Jesus, those I need to forgive.

Think of those people, and in your mind choose to forgive them. Out loud, say the person's name and in Jesus' name release forgiveness to them.

In the name of Jesus, I now forgive you, N (name the person), *for . . .* (say out loud how that person hurt you and how it made you feel). *I choose to let you go now, and I ask you, Jesus, to bless this person. Amen.*

To some the cross is foolishness, but to us being saved it is the power of God. Come to the one who knows, who knows where we have been and what we are like.

It can be a battle of the will: just put your will to work and push through. It was your will that chose unforgiveness, so just do the opposite now. Do you blame God? Just let it go now, and say sorry for your blame.

Some of you may find it helpful to write a letter to the person who hurt you. Write out the fact that you forgive that person, and then destroy the letter. Some may find it helpful to light a candle as a symbol of forgiveness. For others it may be helpful to get some bread and wine and draw a cross, and symbolically receive and release forgiveness. As you take communion for the next few times, bring the person who has hurt you and leave him or her there at the place where you take the bread and wine. Leave that person at the cross.

8: Grieving Absent Parents

In sermons and talks I've heard a lot spoken of the effect on children of not having a father as they grow up – of having an 'absent father'. When I say 'absent', I mean one who is either always away on business, or is based at home but emotionally absent or lacking in communicating love, affection, self-worth and self-esteem. Although the emphasis is always on 'absent fathers', I've discovered from the experience of my own life and from others I've met and prayed with that an 'absent mother' also has a big effect.

Did you know that every book in the Bible apart from the minor prophets mentions fathering? It's mentioned more times than mothering. God calls himself 'Father', but the Bible also tells us that we're made in the image of God – 'male and female he made them', it says of Adam and Eve. Both males and females have hormones associated with the opposite sex.

God calls himself Father, but he also shows us aspects of

his mothering. Because of my past I've felt an ache inside me, an ache that cries out for mothering. Father God has often met me in that need and nurtured me and shown me such tenderness and gentleness.

God's plan was to set humankind in families in such a way that every child would have a mother and father to nurture, love, care and provide for them. He made sure that his own son Jesus was miraculously born into a family with both a mother and a father. A child needs direction from a father. A father brings protection, a father brings affirmation, and a father brings emotional growth. A father shows a son how to be a man, and a father affirms his daughter's femininity.

My son-in-law has both a son and a daughter. He's so hands-on with them, he's a delight to watch. Only a few months after his son Ted was born, Mark was planning all the things he wanted to do with him when Ted was older. When Ted was a couple of weeks old, Mark said to me one day that he was so full of love for Ted that he wanted to kiss him all over! These feelings were so intense that they surprised and even worried Mark, because they felt so big. My reaction was, 'Great! It's what every tiny baby needs – the strong love, bond and affection from its father.' Men often hold back on the display of exuberant feelings for their children. Maybe they're worried that what they're feeling is perverted. As always, we need to look to our motives, and obviously we need actions appropriate to age, but don't let's withdraw from appropriate affection through fear of what others will think.

Sometimes parents have no idea how to show affection to their children. Maybe it was never displayed to them by their own parents, but it can be both caught and taught! We all need to be affirmed by our earthly father – it's one of his jobs. Father God shows us by example. 'This is my Son, whom I love; with him I am well pleased,' is what he said about Jesus in front of a crowd (Matthew 3:17). Jesus hadn't even started his ministry then; he'd done nothing to deserve this affirmation. Nonetheless, his heavenly Father affirmed Jesus as belonging to him and showed him his pleasure.

I had the privilege of watching my grandson being born. It was quite traumatic actually, as he got stuck for a while and had to be helped out into the world with both forceps and a suction cup! When he was born, his eyes were swollen and almost shut, his head was misshapen from the suction cup and his face was very swollen and bruised. That night was such an emotional time that I was too drained to feel anything other than relieved it was all over. The next day, however, an enormous feeling hit me in the chest as I went to lift up my baby grandson Ted. It was an overwhelming love for this little bruised baby. It was so strong that it physically hurt me so that I could hardly breathe.

I wrote little Ted a card for him to read when he was older, a note from me affirming him at his birth, telling him of my love for him and letting him know that our home would always be his home and that he could always come to us if he was ever in need.

Affirmation is such a simple thing. We so need it, but not all of us get it because our parents are either unable or unwilling to give it. In fact, we need affirmation throughout our childhood. I've been amazed watching Ted grow up. From the beginning my daughter and son-in-law have poured affirmation upon him. So much so that at the age of two and a half he was affirming us! 'Well done!' he would say, or, 'Good try!'

If we don't receive affirmation in our childhood, we can become a people-pleaser, or a clown, a self-centred person who seeks attention. I've met people in whom this has become out of control and they've become a compulsive liar or someone with an extreme fantasy life, just because of their need to get attention. In fact, if we become like this, then the reaction we get from people is the opposite of what we desire. People can reject us when all we're seeking is acceptance and affirmation.

Have you seen the television programme *The Office*? The main character David makes me feel so embarrassed for him. He almost shouts out and craves for affirmation. Because he doesn't get it, he affirms himself all the time! Often people on television or the stage who live the life of a clown or a comedian are very sad in real life. Some brilliant comedians have either committed suicide or turned to drugs or drink to cover up their need for affirmation.

The character of Basil Fawlty in *Fawlty Towers* also springs to mind. He so wanted to be seen in the best light, but was constantly failing and covering up his failure, and was often battling against inferiority.

It can make us feel inferior if we're not affirmed as a child. We need to be affirmed in so many ways: in our sexuality, as belonging in our family, and as objects of our parents' pride.

When Jesus was baptised, he heard his heavenly Father say as he came out of the water, 'This is my Son . . . with him I am well pleased.' Our heavenly Father says the same thing to us – he wants to affirm us with these words. We need to hear them but also digest them, let them dwell in us. Let's dissect these words.

This (you, as a person)
is my son. . . (are flesh of my flesh, son or daughter. . .)
with him (with all that you are)
I am (I, your heavenly Father – 'I am' is the name of God, who is always present – am)
well (very – not a little bit, a lot)
pleased (delighted – you give me pleasure)

Father God was telling Jesus that he liked him, he was pleased with him, Jesus gave him pleasure. He tells us that too. If we want to know what the Father is like, we're told in the Bible to look at Jesus. Jesus said, 'I and the Father are one' (John 10:30). If we know Jesus, we know the Father. Look at the relationship Jesus had with his heavenly Father. The Father loves us like he loves Jesus, because Jesus lives inside us; he looks at us with this same love.

My husband Ken and I have two daughters on earth (and two in heaven). We love them with the same love. If our youngest one makes us a cup of coffee, we don't love her more – we can't, it's impossible. We love her because we love her. We don't love her more than her sister and we don't love her more when she does something for us. Yes, it gives us pleasure, but we don't love her more and we don't love her less when she messes up.

With Father God, we don't even have to make him a cup of coffee for him to be pleased with us! He's pleased because he made us and we're made in his image. Making us gave him pleasure. We don't have to do anything to earn it; we can't. Because of Jesus, we can receive the Father's love.

Psalm 68 tells us, 'A father to the fatherless, a defender of widows, is God in his holy dwelling' (v. 5). It also tells us that 'God sets the lonely in families' (v. 6).

What were your earthly mother and father like? Think about them and ask yourself the following questions:

- Did they cuddle me?
- Did they spend time with me?
- Did they talk to me?
- Did they listen to me?
- Did they protect me?
- Did they discipline me?
- Did they affirm me?
- Did they affirm my sexuality?

Now take a look at your answers and acknowledge your real feelings. Face the truth. If you didn't feel accepted by your mother or father, face that truth. If you didn't have your sexuality affirmed, face that fact. Take time now to grieve for the loss of your acceptance and affirmation. Take time out now both to grieve and to forgive those who have hurt you.

In a moment, shut your eyes and think of a favourite childhood place – a place where you felt relaxed and safe, or a place where you enjoyed being. Ask Jesus to be present there with you and to sit beside you, as you would have wanted your father or mother to do. Tell him about your childhood years. Tell him about those teenage years. Tell him what you missed out on. Then tell him about your

LET THE HEALING BEGIN

struggles and your worries. Relax against him and feel his presence. Take time out now and do that.

Have a look at the following chart and tick any of the statements that you think describe your father. Maybe your father was none of these things, so how about your mother? If you had no father, then think of someone who was a dominant father figure in your life, perhaps a grand-father or stepfather.

My father (mother) was:

1. distant and disinterested
2. insensitive and uncaring
3. stern and demanding
4. passive and cold
5. absent or too busy for me
6. impatient or angry
7. mean, cruel or abusive
8. trying to take all the fun out of life
9. controlling or manipulative
10. condemning or unforgiving
11. a perfectionist

Sometimes, because of our view of our earthly parents, we have a wrong view of who our heavenly Father is.

Our heavenly Father is:

1. intimate and involved (Psalm 139:1–18)
2. kind and compassionate (Psalm 103:8–14)
3. accepting (Zephaniah 3:17; Romans 15:7)
4. affectionate (Isaiah 40:11; Hosea 11:3–4)

5. always with me and eager to spend time with me (Jeremiah 31:20; Ezekiel 34:11–16; Hebrews 13:5–6)
6. patient, slow to anger, and pleased with me in Christ (Exodus 34:6; 2 Peter 3:9)
7. loving, gentle and protective of me (Psalm 18:2; Isaiah 42:3; Jeremiah 31:3)
8. trustworthy and wanting to give me a full life (Lamentations 3:22–23; John 10:10; Romans 12:1)
9. full of grace and mercy, and willing to give me the freedom to choose, even when I am wrong (Hebrews 4:15–16)
10. tenderhearted and forgiving – his arms are always open to me (Psalm 130:1–4; Luke 15:17–24)
11. committed to my growth and proud of me as his growing child (Romans 8:28–29; 2 Corinthians 7:4; Hebrews 12:5–11)

Now match up the two charts by the numbers. Look at your view of your earthly parent – for example:

1. distant and disinterested

Then look at the truth about your heavenly Father:

1. intimate and involved (Psalm 139:1–18)

Go back down your list, looking to see how your view of your earthly father or mother may have affected the way you view your heavenly Father. We can think that Father God is like our earthly parent. Let's pray now and renounce the lies that we've accepted concerning the nature of our heavenly Father.

Now read Deuteronomy 32:10–12, part of the Song of
Moses, which to me speaks of both the mothering and the
fathering of God in the symbolic picture of an eagle. The
words are set out below, and I have put in italics my meditation on them.

In a desert land he found him,

> *nothing to drink – thirsty – nothing spiritual to drink in – dry –
> all alone – feeling death close*

in a barren and howling waste.

> *no life – nothing at all – no comfort – no shelter – abandoned*

He shielded him and cared for him;

> *he/she needed shielding in a desert from the sun that burns and
> could kill – no food or drink – Father God as total provider*

he guarded him as the apple of his eye,

> *as someone precious – the best – fully protected*

like an eagle that stirs up its nest

> *it's the mother eagle who does this, who knows it's difficult and*

*painful, but also knows it's the best for her babies – they have to be
pushed out – they cannot stay in the nest – they need to grow up*

and hovers over its young,

*she is waiting and watching, nurturing and encouraging, ready to
help, but allowing them to spread their wings to fly*

that spreads its wings to catch them

*she protects them – wanting them to fly, encouraging them, but
ready in case they fall in flight*

and carries them on its pinions.

*and if they fall, she catches them on her shoulders, between her
wings*

The LORD alone led him;

this is a picture of the Lord showing us the way

no foreign God was with him.

only the Lord could do it

Maybe you were lonely as a child and the last place you
want to be now is with your family. The fact is, God has
put us into a family – the family of God, the church. If you
want to run away from your own family members, then
you have the choice of many people in the church family.
If you're able to, get to know the families in your church.
Offer to babysit for them, and then play football with
their children or take them out to the park. Over the
years, when our children were young, we got to know a lot
of young people who babysat for our children. They
became our friends. One of them ended up choosing our
daughters to be her bridesmaids. We asked another to be
godmother to one of our children. We became their

extended family. The extended family can be a healing place provided by God.

If you were never fathered, get to know some of the father figures in your church. Join a cell group or small group where there are older father figures. Get to know God as your heavenly Father. A really good book on this subject is *The Father Heart of God* by Floyd McClung.

I have previously told you a lot about my mum, but I thought I'd tell you now about my dad. At the time of writing he's 88 and now suffers from dementia and is living in a residential care home. He has always affirmed me. Even now, when he can hardly string two words together that make sense, he affirms me. He strokes my head and shows his love. Up until last year he could tell me he loved me, and he thanked me and told me I was wonderful. This wasn't a one-off thing – he did it regularly. I'm so thankful to God that I've always known my dad loves me. His dad died when my dad was 14 years old, but he always knew that he had loved him and also that his mum loved him. He passed this on to my brother and me.

I've made many mistakes as a parent, but one thing I know that I *have* done right is that I've always made it a point to tell our children that I love them and that I'm proud of them. I'm sure that because of this, they don't hold back in pointing out to me the times and ways in which I've let them down. This is good, because it means that I can say 'sorry' and try to put things right.

We need to hear 'I love you' and 'I'm proud of you' from our parents. If we haven't heard these affirmations, then more than ever we need to hear them from our loving heavenly Father. Let's pray about that now.

Let's pray

Father God, we ask you in Jesus' name that you would show us how much you love us deep inside. Show us in many ways how proud you are of us because you made us. Where we weren't affirmed, show us by the power of the Holy Spirit in these days ahead – whisper to us your approval. Show us when we've done wrong, too – we want to be able to come to you and be honest about our wrongdoing without fear. Thank you that we are acceptable to you because of Jesus. Amen.

A few years ago, I remember praying for a young guy I'll call Peter. Do you remember the story I told about him in Chapter 2? At the age of five he was left at home alone one evening to look after his two-year-old sister, who was asleep in her cot. His mum and dad were partying down the road somewhere – he didn't even know where. The baby woke up and started to cry. The little five-year-old was scared because he couldn't make his little baby sister stop crying. He left the baby in the cot and went down the street, crying and looking for his parents. He didn't know where to find them, so he kept knocking on the doors until he discovered where they were partying. Their response was not one of remorse, but one of anger, because they'd been disturbed. Throughout his life, Peter's parents abused him emotionally and neglected him. Peter took on the responsibility of emotionally parenting his sister and decided to live a life of survival at all costs.

Story after story Peter told me of his abusive childhood, but he never showed any emotion or feelings. After every story he said, 'That's just the way it was.'

On the one hand, he seemed to accept what had happened to him, but his suicidal thoughts and his depression told another story. His loss and grief about his emotionally absent parents must have been huge, but he couldn't admit it to himself, so he definitely wouldn't or couldn't admit it to those of us who were praying for him. He was in denial.

Over the next few weeks, whenever we met up to pray, he would always say the same thing in response to the traumatic stories he told us: 'That's just the way it was.' When we prayed for him he kept his eyes open, as if too frightened to shut them because of what he might see. I could so easily have done the emotion for him! I could have cried buckets, and I felt so angry at the neglect and abuse he had suffered over the years.

His parents made him feel worthless and stupid; he had never been affirmed in anything. His parents always put him down; his mother was an emotional wreck. If Peter were to admit everything, all his pain would be too much for him to bear, so he chose to be in denial in the hope that it would go away. But of course it didn't – it just gave him sleepless nights and dark thoughts about ending his life.

After a few more weeks of this, I started to goad him. I believe this was God's idea rather than mine, as I would never normally do such a thing! I certainly don't ever recommend doing such a thing as usual practice. I said, 'It was really good, wasn't it, Peter, that your mum and dad never showed you affection? It was good that they left you on your own so much to look after your little sister. It was great that you had all that responsibility for the baby and everything was made to look your fault. You liked never having a hug or a kiss. You liked being left on your own.' I went on and on, hardly believing what I was hearing coming out of my mouth. It just poured out of me.

Peter was starting to respond through body language. He started squirming and moving as if he was uncomfortable.

Then I said, 'You like all this stuff inside you, don't you? This pain, this self-hatred?'

Suddenly he cracked and broke through all of his denial with a loud shout: 'No! I don't like it, but it's all I have!'

Then Peter sobbed and sobbed. The crack had appeared and there was no stopping it now. He sobbed out his years of agony, pain, frustration and self-hatred. At last he'd admitted to himself that he did have pain – he owned it. He cried because he knew that the only way forward was to express it, to feel it and to let it go. He cried because he was having to admit that his parents were cruel, that they'd abused him, that they hadn't shown him any love, hadn't given him any attention.

It was only when he admitted his loss and his lack of parenting that he could allow his heavenly Father access to his heart. Peter was at last able to allow Jesus to come and give him what he'd never had: love. The Lord continued to minister his love to Peter throughout the summer during a time away from our church. The next time I saw him, he looked so different. He looked radiant with the love of Jesus. I was so pleased to hear that he was entering full-time Christian evangelistic work, touring around telling other young people his testimony about the love of his heavenly Father.

> Praise be to the God and Father of our Lord Jesus Christ, the Father of compassion and the God of all comfort, who comforts us in all our troubles. (2 Corinthians 1:3–4)

In the Bible we're told about the kingdom of heaven being like a lost coin. When we haven't had something in our upbringing that we should have had, like a parent who loves us, then, like the person looking for that lost coin, we search and search, trying to find it. We fret over it, long for it, crave for it, and we'll keep searching for it. Sometimes we'll try to put things in its place, either to cover up the lack or to substitute something else for it. But that thing never satisfies – it can't. It's a love-shaped hole, and only Father God can fill it.

Jesus can take us as that deprived child and take us to his Father, our heavenly Father. Our God is a loving God, a loving Father who delights in all that he has made. Have you ever seen a cat basking in the sunshine? It's relaxed, abandoned, stretched out. That's exactly how we're meant to be in our heavenly Father's arms – lying there in total trust, safety and abandonment. Our Father in heaven sees everything, and we are a constant delight to him.

I see our grandson and granddaughter nearly every day. I look forward to it. If I don't see them for a couple of days, I really miss them. I don't blame them if I don't see them, neither am I angry with them. It's just that I'm even more delighted when I do see them. How much more must Father God feel this when we come to him! His arms are open wide. The problem is, we can't run into those arms because our own arms are too full of other things.

A few years ago, Ken and I met a young man when we were involved in a Soul Survivor conference abroad. I told you a little bit about him in Chapter 2. Andy had a severe compulsive disorder and was taking medication for it. As we prayed for him, I sensed that he had a deep grief that was unresolved. As I questioned him, we discovered that he'd never known his earthly father. In fact, he was illegitimate. Andy told us his story: his mother had an affair with a married man who was the pastor of her church. As soon as the pastor knew his mistress was pregnant (with Andy), he left his wife, his church and his town, never to be seen again.

As we prayed, I realised that Andy held such a big anger against his father for leaving him, and he was so ashamed that he was the by-product of both his mother's and his father's sin. His father not only sinned against his wife, his mistress and his son, but he also sinned against his congregation, the body of Christ. The story that came into my mind from the Bible was the one about the man who had been born blind and who was accused of being 'steeped in sin at his birth'. Andy carried this shame every day and it affected him in a big way. It made him so anxious that he had to check everything compulsively several times to make sure he didn't make a mistake. This lessened his anxiety in one way, but made him more anxious in another way, because he was also ashamed of his compulsive actions.

Andy longed for a father, but he couldn't relate to his heavenly Father. His heavenly Father had his arms open wide to Andy, but Andy's arms were already full. They were full of shame, full of guilt, full of blame, full of pain, full of a feeling of victimhood. I asked him to bring all this stuff in his arms and lay it down at the feet of Jesus. He said, 'I can't. What would I have left then? I wouldn't know who I was.'

'Yes you would,' I said. 'You would know that you belonged to your heavenly Father. But the thing is, you haven't met him yet.'

Andy struggled and wrestled with these decisions. All this stuff in his arms had been his identity for 23 years. Then, in Jesus' name, he chose to give it all up and chose to forgive his earthly father for sinning against him and leaving him.

He then got free of all those things he was carrying, one by one. Then I said to him, 'Now take Jesus' hand and ask him to take you to your heavenly Father.'

We watched Andy extend his arms and call out, 'Father!' It was wonderful to watch.

What happened next was something only God himself could orchestrate. We were standing outside a marquee, and inside 300 people were gathered for worship. At the very moment Andy held his arms out to his heavenly Father, Matt Redman started to sing 'The Father's Song'! Andy started crying and laughing at the same time. His heavenly Father was welcoming him in with singing.

As Andy continued to receive acceptance and healing, Ken gave him his hanky to wipe away his tears. 'Here,' he said, 'take this as if from your heavenly Father.' Andy wiped his eyes and nose on the hanky. I was so touched by this demonstration of a typical gesture from a father to a son. We had tissues, but Ken felt it to be a symbolic act that would bring healing. And it did. Andy laundered the hanky and kept it as a reminder of the healing he had received from Father God.

A few weeks later, I received an email from Andy saying that he had been to see his doctor and was off all medication for his obsessive-compulsive disorder. I saw him a year later and he was still free from this disorder.

Just think of yourself as a child; maybe imagine a memory or a photograph of yourself with your family sitting around a dining table. Have a look around the table. Can you see a parent or parents who loved and affirmed you? Did you have two parents who did that? Then thank God for them. If you didn't, then let Jesus take you by the hand. Lay down the things that hinder you from knowing God as your heavenly Father. Forgive those who have hurt you. Have empty arms. Let Jesus take you and lead you to your heavenly Father. Climb up onto his lap; let Father God affirm you now. You are safe with him. Think about those things you were never affirmed in – your ability, your worth, your position in the family as son or daughter, your belonging. Ask Father God to parent you. He is able to give back what you didn't have. What has been stolen away he can restore to you. Let him do it. *He wants to.*

9: **Suffering Loss**

Throughout life we suffer loss and we grieve about those losses. Grief isn't just about someone whom we love, dying; it's about all sorts of losses that can occur as we grow up, and if we don't grieve for these losses healthily they may still be felt throughout our life. Some losses are small and we're able to grieve naturally without them causing us too much heartache, but others can cause stumbling blocks to wholeness. How have we coped with some of the losses we suffered in our past?

What sort of losses do I mean? Look at the list below and see if you have suffered any of them, or add your own.

- Death of someone close, whom you loved
- Divorce (your parents or your own)
- Sexual abuse
- Physical abuse
- Emotional abuse
- Neglect
- Amputation of a limb

- Moving house at a significant age
- Always moving from place to place
- Fire that destroyed part or all of your home
- Bankruptcy
- Imprisonment of a parent
- Death of a pet
- Leaving home to get married
- Broken engagement
- Redundancy
- Serious illness
- Child leaving home
- Failing exams
- Parent with terminal illness
- Alcoholic parent
- Friends moving away

Grief comes when part of our life is lost or we are robbed of it, as in the case of abuse. There are plans that will never come to pass and things that we'll never have again. It means enormous changes taking place, either around us or inside us. When we're young, some of these losses can make a huge impact on our lives and we can find it difficult to move on. It's as if we're still stuck in that time of loss and grief. Here are a few other examples of loss:

Moving house

As a child aged ten, I remember moving from the home I'd always known to another house in the same district. We left a safe, cosy home and moved to a house that smelled funny and was dirty. Most of my life was without change and very routine, as we didn't own a car and my mum was usually too ill, so we never went anywhere much. When we moved, I had to change schools. The one I'd left had been just opposite our house and everyone had known us there. It was very strange and scary to go somewhere that was unfamiliar and to be amongst strangers. Up until a couple of years ago, I still dreamed about our old home and the dreams always contained good vibes. Whenever I dreamed about the next house, it was always with anxious feelings.

My new primary school was so different. One of the difficult things that I remember was having to play net-ball. This was an unfamiliar game to me. Everyone else but me knew how to play. All the children kept telling me I was stupid because I didn't know how to play it. No one ever wanted me to be on their team, because I always dropped the ball or ran to the wrong end of the court. There seemed to be no one to ask how to play.

All the rules at the new school were different, too. At my old school I was a very confident and well-known person; at the new school I shrank back, and became fearful of try-ing new things. At the old school all the teachers knew about my mum having agoraphobia, and they understood why she never came to visit the school. I felt such a loss of identity, and a loss of all that was familiar and safe. It was as if so much had been taken away from me. My brother Terry and I were very upset about our new home for a long time, as we felt robbed of some things that were precious to us.

Although all that sounds such a small thing to lose, to a child something like moving house can seem enormous. During the last 25 years I've met many people who moved house many times as children because of a parent's career or other circumstances. Mostly these losses have had a huge impact on their lives. Their loss caused them insecurity and a loss of identity. Grief is a normal response to the loss of any significant person, object or opportunity.

Divorce

A lot of people know about the grief and loss of divorce. For many I've met, the moment when they were told by a parent that they were leaving the family home is a memory that's etched into their emotions. Some never guessed what was coming, as they thought everything was OK. For others, the constant rowing, shouting and in some cases violence was a prelude to many years spent listening, hiding and watching from the safety of the stairs. As a child suffering this sort of grief, it's like being torn in two. Which parent deserves the child's allegiance, as he or she loves them both? It's usually surprising which parent is chosen, as it's often the one who causes the child the most grief.

Although I don't know what it feels like to be a child of divorced parents, here are some of the losses I've observed that people suffer through divorce:

For an adult
- Loss of status
- Loss of companionship
- Loss of wealth
- Loss of security
- A sense of guilt
- A sense of shame

- Extreme anger
- Low self-esteem

For a child
- Loss of home and familiarity
- Loss of family unit
- Loss of security
- Loss affecting self-worth and self-esteem
- A sense of shame
- A sense of sorrow
- A sense of guilt
- Extreme anger

Abuse

The loss and grief caused by the abuse of a child is extreme, even if the abuse only occurred once. Neglect, and physical, sexual and emotional abuse can produce the following:

- Loss of innocence
- Physical and emotional loss
- Loss of relationship with perpetrator
- Loss of security and safety
- Loss of self-worth
- Loss of trust
- Loss of identity
- Loss of peace
- Loss of sexual awakening

Something has been stolen from the child. Jesus said, 'If anyone causes one of these little ones who believe in me to sin, it would be better for him to be thrown into the sea with a large millstone tied around his neck' (Mark 9:42). Jesus knows what harm it does to little children when they are sinned against. He hates it. He will see to it that it doesn't go unpunished.

* * *

Although grief and loss are so very painful, if we allow the pain to surface and we work through it, there can be some surprising results. Jesus said, 'Unless a grain of wheat falls to the ground and dies, it remains only a single seed. But if it dies, it produces many seeds' (John 12:24). If we allow it, growth will come from our losses.

In our family we have suffered a lot of losses in the past four years. Just over four years ago, my husband Ken was struck down with a very rare and serious illness. Initially it was thought that he had sciatica or a compressed disc. After six weeks of agony, he was finally taken by ambulance to hospital. He was in so much agony that the ambulance men said it was best if he tried to crawl down the stairs, as it would be less jarring and painful for him. Beth and I went into the garden so that we couldn't hear his screams of pain. We travelled at a snail's pace behind the ambulance as it crawled along, avoiding all the bumps and holes in the road.

After X-rays and a CT scan, Ken was diagnosed as having discitis. This was an infection in his disc, a ball of pus that had eaten away at his disc and was now eating away at his vertebrae. He also had septicaemia, and so it was a race against time. They gave him so much morphine during the five weeks that he was in hospital, the most that they could give without him being unconscious, but he was still in agony and couldn't move and had to lie on his side. For six weeks we didn't know if he would have to have an operation that could potentially paralyse him, as he had osteomyelitis. Some people came to visit him, but failed to recognise him, so they turned around and went to walk out. He'd lost almost two stone in weight, he'd grown a full beard, and his hair was so long that it stuck up high in the air because it hadn't been washed for ten weeks, as he was in too much agony for it to be touched. When he finally came home, we didn't know if he would ever walk again. Everything in our lives came to a standstill for about six months. Even after this time, Ken still couldn't sit up in an armchair and had to lean over the side. It was such an incredible shock to all of us, as Ken hadn't been ill in 34 years of marriage apart from the flu for two weeks!

When Ken was in hospital during those agonising weeks, as we wondered if he was going to live or die, or if he was going to be in a wheelchair for the rest of his life, I used to shout out to Father God my pain and frustration: 'You'd better have something good coming out of this!' At other times I'd shout out, 'This is so *hard*! I hate it. This is like dying inside.' Every night when I got home and went into our bedroom, it was as if Ken had died. The whole house felt empty. I wasn't used to him being away, as we only spent one or two nights a year apart.

I knew the verse from Romans 8:28: 'And we know that in all things God works for the good of those who love him, who have been called according to his purpose.' This was in my head every time I drove to the hospital, but there seemed to be nothing good about what was happening. At times it made me angry, but I knew I had nothing else to hold onto, so I held onto this hope. It was frightening, it was lonely, and I felt as if my head was only just above the water.

At the same time as all this was happening to Ken, I was in the middle of a building project at church. I was overseeing the conversion of a factory into our new church building, and there was a deadline as some people in the church were planning a production of the musical *Joseph* and had sold loads of tickets. I was under so much pressure, because I was the only one who was handling a lot of the decisions. Ken was the accountant, and he was the only one who knew if we could afford the various costs. Suddenly I felt all alone, as I didn't know what the finances were and Ken was so high on morphine that he was in no state to make any decisions!

The telephone was constantly ringing, with people enquiring either about Ken's illness or about the building project. I was spending five hours a day at the warehouse and eight hours at the hospital, then going home to work on the computer. I fell into bed at 2 a.m. and got up at 6 a.m.

During the first week of Ken's illness I also started to teach a course at church entitled 'Freedom From Past Hurts'. How ironic, now that I was hurting too!

As if this wasn't enough, our youngest daughter was writing her dissertation for her degree, and because she's dyslexic she needed my help with proofreading.

Also while Ken was in hospital, our house was being rethatched. I couldn't reschedule it, as it had been booked in to be done for a year. Good thatchers are difficult to get.

Our house was so dark inside, because we had double scaffolding all around the outside. This made the house very cold, although it was 80 degrees outside!

To cap it all, at the same time as the thatchers were there we had to have our flat roof refelted. This became an emergency job, because the thatchers needed it to be done quickly as it was holding up their work. Unfortunately, that day we had some torrential rain! I came home from the hospital late at night and discovered that rain had come through the roof in five places. My bed was soaking wet, as was the carpet.

During this same time our cat was unwell and very elderly and our 15-year-old dog developed a rapid illness, and both had to be put down.

As you can imagine, everything became overwhelming. I felt very alone and isolated. During all this anguish I started to thank God for tears, as I cried every day. Sometimes I cried three or four times a day – it was my only relief. The house felt so very big, and so did all the things that were happening around me. It felt as if Ken had died, but in fact he was still alive although there was no change in his condition. Week after week, we didn't know what the future held. This lasted for about nine months. We didn't plan anything. We just lived a day at a time.

During this time I learned to submit to the Lord. Everything was beyond my control; there was nothing I could change by my own efforts. I felt such a grief for our life that used to be, such loss for the person that Ken used to be. I learned to value each day and to take pleasure in minute things.

Then came the day when Ken first stood up from his bed (he couldn't sit up, but had to go from a lying position) and tried his first step. It seemed miraculous at the time. It was a big occasion when he first walked a few steps with a walking frame. It was marvellous on the day when he walked as far as the back door of our house to get his first breath of fresh air. It was like a holiday on the day when he managed to walk down a small step to lie down in the garden.

Our first major treat was when we had afternoon tea lying down in the garden. We'd never sat in our garden before, as we'd always been too busy. This became the highlight of our day – afternoon tea for 20 minutes (this was the longest he could bear in this position).

Then friends with whom we'd lost touch started to visit us, and we valued this as another highlight in our day.

I struggled with the loss of freedom, as I could only go out for a short stretch of time and Ken was always anxious about how long I'd be and exactly when I'd be coming back. Six months is a long time. We knew that this illness was going to affect our lives for a very long time, barring another miracle. The consultant said that it would take at least two years for the bones to fuse together, and Ken would be in pain for that long.

Life was very different for the next couple of years as Ken recovered from the physical side of his illness. Four years on, he still feels stiff and achy and isn't able to do some of the physical things that he used to do. He also had to face the mental and emotional side of his recovery.

The whole experience has had some life-changing results for us as a couple, as growth has come and is still coming from this awful time. We made decisions about our future and about what we did with our time. We make more time for each other. We value even more the things that surround us. I used to be too busy with 'the Lord's work' to be thankful for our lovely home and garden. I became even more thankful for our family and friends. This difficult time showed us who were our friends and who were our acquaintances. The things that I had in the past classed as materialistic were the very things that Jesus used to bless us with! It was a humbling time too. I had to do all the driving for about a year, and I learned from my back-seat driver how bad a driver I am! I had to learn to live in 'the now', in today, instead of living in tomorrow.

Although this was a horrific time to live through, I know that our lives are more enriched now – we're even closer as a married couple and as a family unit. If we allow the following verse to happen in our lives, we will know the fruit of it:

> Because we know that suffering produces perseverance; perseverance, character; and character, hope. And hope does not disappoint us, because God has poured out his love into our hearts by the Holy Spirit, whom he has given us. (Romans 5:3–5)

Suffering

We like suffering to be on our own terms, don't we? In fact, at times we even seek after it, for instance having our ears pierced or our body tattooed. How about bungee jumping, or extreme sports, or going to the gym? We assess the risk and go for it, knowing in part the level of suffering and pain we will endure. We mainly choose (apart from childbirth) to put ourselves through it, so we only have ourselves to blame. If we can't understand it, then we don't want it.

Sometimes it can feel as if God is making us hurt. The fact is, Father God hates to see us hurt. No father who loves his child wants to see that child hurt and in pain. Our Father God allowed his only Son not only to suffer the horror of torture and the agonising pain of crucifixion, but to take the whole sin of the world and its pain and suffering onto his shoulders. He not only allowed it, he watched it. Can you imagine what that must have been like, to send your own son to be tortured and to die?

As a parent it's a painful thing to watch when you take your child for inoculations. The baby has a tiny arm and you see this big needle going into it. The baby usually screams. Why do we allow our baby to be given pain? We allow it because we know that this pain is nothing compared to the bigger pain we're saving that baby from.

God doesn't give us pain. He allows it to happen, just like parents allow their children to be given pain. Jesus allowed his friend Lazarus to suffer and die, and then he allowed himself to be misunderstood, because he knew what he was going to do next.

I think it's strange that we so quickly ask the question, 'Why does God allow such suffering?' but are so slow to ask the question, 'Why do I continue to sin and cause God such suffering and sorrow?' He made us a perfect world to live in, with no pain, suffering or sorrow, but we know that if we'd been in the same situation as Adam and Eve we would have given in to temptation just the same. I believe that sometimes the reason why we suffer is that we sin or that we live in a fallen and broken world. One day we'll be in a place where we're promised there will be no tears or sorrow.

Our big question is often, 'Did God do this to me?' I don't know all the answers, but I do know this: what Satan means for harm God uses to bring us good. There are circumstances in which Satan tries to strike us down and tries to hinder us and stop us. Satan tries to wipe us out, but God limits what he can do.

About a year after Ken became ill, I rediscovered these words of Jesus:

> 'Simon, Simon, Satan has asked to sift you [the footnote says the Greek is plural] as wheat. But I have prayed for you, Simon, that your faith may not fail. And when you have turned back, strengthen your brothers.' (Luke 22:31–32)

Throughout Ken's illness I thought over and over, 'How can he bear this? It's such pain and agony, even with the medication.' (He was taking 30 pills a day.) It wasn't until I found this verse that I realised. It wasn't just our friends and church members who were praying for Ken, it was Jesus himself who was praying that Ken's faith would not fail. Ken was unable to pray during this time – he couldn't even think. In that verse Jesus was saying, 'And when you return to me. . .' He knows that when we're suffering and being sifted, we sometimes withdraw from him, but he doesn't blame us. He's praying that we'll return and after that we'll strengthen others, because we understand what they're going through.

Sometimes our suffering happens because of the sin of

others. But in all things nothing can separate us from the love of God that is in Christ Jesus, and God can work together all things for good for those who love him. We need to know that God is in control. We also need to know that Jesus is familiar with suffering and acquainted with our sorrows. He understands.

Take time out now to think through times of loss or suffering. Did it feel as if God was punishing you? Did you withdraw from him? Did you blame him?

Let's pray

Holy Spirit, the Comforter, please come and surface my deep sense of loss and suffering. Please forgive me, Jesus, for the times when I've blamed you for my loss. Enable me to grieve for what I've lost and what I've been robbed of. I choose to submit these things to you now (name them). *Restore me, and what Satan meant for evil, turn it into good. Where I've turned away from you, I'm sorry and choose to trust you. Please come and heal me. I ask, Lord Jesus, that you will look upon my suffering and enable me to persevere and endure. Build my character and fill me with your hope, Lord. Show me the times when you were praying for me in my suffering. Forgive me when I stopped having faith in you to rescue me. I put myself in your hands. Please come, Holy Spirit, and bring to the surface those losses that I've buried. Show me the good things and the growth that you have brought. I bring my losses to you at the cross now, Jesus. You know the agony of my soul. Cover me with your hand of protection. Thank you that you are good and more than able to heal this pain. Amen.*

LET THE HEALING BEGIN

Look at the following psalm. I've put in my own meditation underneath every line. Let the Holy Spirit speak to you through it.

A journey through Psalm 23

The LORD is my shepherd,

That means I am his sheep, imagine his voice and follow him, trust him to look after me. He is in control so I don't have to be.

I shall not be in want.

He will take care of all my needs so I don't have to worry. He will never leave me wanting.

He makes me lie down in green pastures,

Green pastures, a fresh place, close to food, a good place to be, looking at creation, lying down looking up at the sky. When I am lying down I can't fall anywhere. I am at rest and peace here.

he leads me beside quiet waters,

Why? You lead me because I need to be led, I want to follow. It is calming beside still waters, another provision of yours, Lord. I want to leave the troubled waters and walk beside the still waters. I will look upon these still waters; they are refreshing to my soul.

he restores my soul.

Oh yes, restore my grieving soul. My eyes need your restoring, all that I have seen, all that has gone down into my soul. I know it takes time. Thank you, Lord, that you can do it.

He guides me

He shows the way, the only way. I can trust his way. I choose to trust your way, Lord.

in paths of righteousness

In ways of holiness, you are righteous, you have the breastplate of righteousness. I can trust the path you set before me to lead me out of suffering and loss.

for his name's sake.

Because of who he is. Your name is the greatest name, a wonderful name.

Even though I walk through the valley of the shadow of death,

It's only the valley of the shadow of death, it isn't death itself. A valley is a low place, but a valley passes through – comes out on the other side of the mountain – the mountain casts the shadow. I try to run through the valley, but have only enough strength to walk. Some days I have only the strength to crawl.

I will fear no evil,

The enemy wants me to fear evil – the shadow of death. The dark valley makes me fearful, but I will declare that I will fear no evil. Why?

for you are with me;

I will declare this, oh God, to myself, to the devil, to anyone who will hear: you are with me. In my grief you are with me, along the path you are with me, in the darkness of the night you are with me. You will never leave me. I stand on this promise.

your rod and your staff, they comfort me.

Sometimes a shepherd's crook rescues – grabs sheep and lambs around the neck, stops them from falling. Sometimes the rod prods them to move them on, out of danger into a safe place. The staff is used to make sure that the ground ahead isn't too boggy or full of big holes that trip the sheep up or break their legs. Knowing and sensing that you are doing these things comforts me.

You prepare a table before me in the presence of my enemies.

LET THE HEALING BEGIN

Overflowing blessing from things meant for our harm – God turns them into a feast of blessing. Thank you for the table you set before me, a table full of good things, things that you want to share with me.

You anoint my head with oil;
my cup overflows.

Blessing after blessing, almost too much to take in.

Surely goodness and love

Jesus. . .

will follow me

. . .will be on my case. . .

all the days of my life,

. . .all the days, all the days of my life.

and I will dwell in the house of the LORD for ever.

A dwelling place, my Lord's house, a forever place, a place of rest, a place of restoration, a place of healing, a place with him.

Death

Death occurred in the Garden of Eden after Adam and Eve sinned. Animals were killed and their skins were used to cover the nakedness of Adam and Eve, to cover their shame.

Have you noticed on the television how death is mostly portrayed in one of three ways? It's generally presented as horrific, as in the news; as unreal, as in movies or cartoons; or as something funny, as in situation comedies.

Nothing we're ever taught seems to prepare us for the death of someone close. At school, were you taught anything about death or how to cope with grief or loss? At home, were we taught about it or prepared for it before it happened? At church, are we taught how painful it will be when someone we love dies?

In my home as a child I heard this sort of comment: 'Mrs Collins has just lost her husband.' I used to wonder about that – when would she 'find' him again? Another equally confusing comment I overheard was, 'Mr Bowen's wife has passed away,' or perhaps, 'The butcher has popped his clogs at last!' What does all that mean to a child?

We seem to avoid the word 'death' at all costs. We try to pretty the word up and make it into something far away from us, but we can't. No wonder we're not prepared for death when it comes close by.

Children can be very affected by grief, and also by guilt. Imagine, for example, that a child knows Mummy is pregnant and wants Mummy to play or wants to sit on Mummy's lap, but then Mummy says 'no', because of the baby in her tummy. The child can then get angry at both Mummy and the baby, and wants Mummy as she was before. Maybe the child thinks, 'I hate that baby! I wish it wasn't here.' What if Mummy then miscarries the baby? The child is left with a huge guilt, thinking it was his or her fault that the baby died. This can obviously also be true of other situations concerning death.

Grieving the death of a loved one isn't easy. As Christians we sometimes try to make it into something beautiful when the person grieving isn't yet ready. When we encounter death, we face an irreversible, unalterable situation that we're powerless to change. That's why it's so hard to bear.

LET THE HEALING BEGIN

Children can have unresolved fears about death. Our own five-year-old daughter Alex waited a year after her sister drowned before she was ready to face some of this fear and allow some of the disturbing things that had happened to surface. Before this time it must have been too frightening, so her mind just pushed it back to a place where she couldn't look at it. It was another ten years before other aspects relating to that time were ready to be dealt with.

Even as Christians, knowing that death has been swallowed up in victory, we can find the loss of a loved one devastating and overwhelming.

Grief

We can grieve as young as two years old. What is grief? We're all different and so we grieve in different ways, but we dip in and out of the following emotions: shock, euphoria, emptiness, lostness, guilt, anger, regrets, fear, anxiety, nightmares, forgetfulness, loneliness, the need to be alone, depression, insomnia, headaches. We can go through a variety of these states in one day, or for one day we can feel just one of them intensely. After a while we have good days and bad days. Then we can have more good days than bad days. At times it seems as if we're in a very dark place, just like the psalmist describes – the valley of the shadow of death. Suddenly, out of the blue, we can revisit any of these big emotions and it can feel as if we've taken one step forward and two steps back. Finally we'll come to that place of being able to say goodbye, this has happened, this is part of my life, it will never be forgotten, but it's no longer in the foreground, I can start to rebuild my life again and go on.

Problems can occur when we haven't resolved some of these big feelings and we get stuck. That's when we need some help to work through them. Counselling is a good way, especially bereavement counselling. Ask your doctor or go to the library to see what's available in your area. Talking things over can help surface those big feelings and can help us make choices that lead to healing. As things surface we can then ask a friend to pray with us, asking the Holy Spirit, the Comforter and Counsellor, to heal us.

One of the big questions we ask when grief occurs is 'Why? Why? Why?' The question becomes so huge in our mind. There is never an answer to this question. In the book *When Heaven is Silent*, Ronald Dunn implies that this question is about our anger, that we're feeling angry especially towards God, that we're blaming him for what has happened: 'Why did you do this to me, God? Why did you let this happen?' I suggest that this is the reason why we never hear a reply to that question. Instead we should be asking, 'What now? What now, Lord?'

At times grief feels like a big black hole. Before I became a Christian, I described my own grief as like being down a big, deep, slimy pit with no way of getting out. I didn't know the God of the slimy pit then! So what happened? Did God pull me out? No – Jesus came down into the pit with me and positioned his body so that I could stand on him and climb out.

In the Bible Jesus is described by Isaiah as 'a man of sorrows, and familiar with suffering . . . [who] took up our infirmities and carried our sorrows' (Isaiah 53:3–4). We can't do it alone, and we were never meant to.

LET THE HEALING BEGIN

Grief can be a depth of agony or despair, an emptiness, a nothingness stretching before us, a blackness sucking us down. At first it's like a gaping wound, and when healed it leaves its mark. We think it's all healed and then something can happen, maybe to someone else, and it can touch that scar and can cause us tears once more.

A few years ago, I felt thrown into the world of suffering, grief and loss once more. Our daughter was expecting twins and went into premature labour three months too soon. She was on holiday in Dorset and as soon as we received the telephone call we rushed down to see her in hospital. Six of us camped out at the hospital as they fought for one and a half days to prevent the labour continuing. But they couldn't stop it, and so for the next two days Alex was in labour. Our emotions went up and down, through fear and hope, anxiety and wonder, as we thought about these two little boys who were fighting to be born.

Finally little Harry and Charlie were born, perfect in every way, but so tiny – just one and a half pounds each. They were so beautiful. Harry, who seemed to be the strongest, only lived for one and a half days, and Charlie followed him aged two days.

Initially, when I heard by telephone that Alex had gone into labour, I rushed out into the street (I was in a meeting at the time) and screamed at God, 'Please God, don't let this happen to her like it happened to me!' I'd had a stillborn baby, such a difficult loss to come to terms with, and I so wanted Alex to see her babies alive.

Do you know what my daughter and son-in-law call their twin boys? They call them 'our miracle boys' –

because they lived, and they fought and fought for the short time that they lived in this world. Of course their parents' loss was so great and so deep. For me, I was thrown back into this familiar place of grief and sorrow. My old scars were knocked open. I couldn't bear that my daughter was suffering the sort of pain I had suffered, and I was experiencing feelings from the past that I thought were healed and long gone. I also felt that I was letting my daughter down, as I wanted to be supportive to her in her great time of need. I had to give myself permission to feel the pain and not feel guilty.

At first I felt numb and empty. I couldn't pray or read my Bible. I used to go into my room and just say to Jesus, 'I am here,' and then I would just sit there with nothing to give and unable to receive. This went on for a couple of months. I thought I would always be like this.

Then I had a dream: I was in my car, parked by the side of the road, using my mobile phone. To the left of me, lying down in the road, I could see this huge moose, seemingly dead. I started to press 999 on my phone to get help, when suddenly the moose started to come alive. He rose up, gnashing his teeth and looking ferocious. Quite disturbed, I got out of my car and headed towards my family, who were standing by the side of the road. I placed myself in front of them and also our dog, who was barking at the moose. The moose was now in front of us, the most beautiful animal I'd ever seen. It was enormous and majestic and wild, gnashing his teeth. As I looked at the moose, I felt no fear as I realised that the moose wasn't trying to be scary, he was just being who he was, big and wild. I felt such an enormous love for this moose. Suddenly I started to sing and speak out in tongues in an unknown language, and I started moving and dancing like the woman who appears in the stage show *The Lion King*. As I started doing this, I realised that I was communicating with the moose. It was wonderful. The moose started to lead me away and I followed, singing and dancing and communicating with him. Then I woke up with the thought of Aslan from *The Lion, the Witch and the Wardrobe* in my head. The children asked, 'Is he safe?' 'No,' the answer came, 'but he is good.' In my mind in the dream I related more to the fact that what I'd seen was wild, so my question would have been, 'Is he wild?' 'Yes, and he is good.' 'Is he tame?' 'No, but he is good.'

I looked in a book for information about the moose, as I'd never seen one except in my dream. I was amazed to learn how huge they actually are. It said in the book that they're enormous creatures, dangerous, but they go into ponds and eat water lilies!

I thought about the dream when I awoke. It was so vivid, the first dream that I'd had for months. The moose was wild, he wasn't trying to harm me, he was just being who he was. I went to see a friend and described the dream to her, hoping she would have an interpretation for me. As I told her, however, I began to cry as I started to interpret it myself. I so missed communicating with God, I was so numb that I felt no connection to him any more. I realised that the moose represented God. At the start of the dream the moose was seemingly dead. My view was that God was powerless to stop what had happened, and I had stopped trusting him. Suddenly his beauty and wild-ness was revealed to me. I couldn't tame him, he was so much bigger than me, but from my guts I needed to communicate with him – not politely, but with my big feelings of grief, telling him what I felt about him allowing what had happened to my daughter and her husband and those beautiful little boys.

My friend assured me that the time would come and I would know when it was right to let out my pain and go for it.

A few days later I was driving my car down a country lane, when suddenly into my head came the loud word 'Now!' I quickly turned into an even smaller lane and switched off the engine. I screamed and screamed out my pain to God. I shouted in English, I shouted in tongues. From the depths of my guts I let him have my anguish, my horror, my disappointment, until I was absolutely exhausted. I would love to tell you that at that moment I heard the voice of God telling me wondrous things, but I didn't. All I heard was a heavy silence. But I didn't feel numb any more. I could feel.

I would never know the answer to my 'Why?', but I knew I could trust this big, wild God. He was a God I would never understand, but I didn't need to. That's the point: I never would understand him and his ways. He was scary, but in my eyes he was magnified. It was comforting for me to know that although I didn't understand what had happened, he did. How important it is to be honest with our God in our pain, to tell him like it really is. We need to give a voice to our pain and agony, and not be polite Christians. The psalmists aren't very polite with the Lord: they let out their frustration and anger. We often read their words in a very polite voice, when we should be ranting and raving.

In the Bible we're shown so many people who suffered. Job, for example, suffered loss of health, grief from the death of family members, and the loss of his wealth. Abraham moved away from his country. Jacob mourned the loss of Joseph. David grieved over the death of Jonathan, and he grieved for the death of his child caused by his own sin. Mary, who bore Jesus, endured the sight of his suffering and his death.

Mary suffered incredible losses: the loss of her reputation when she became pregnant with Jesus, the loss of not having her own family around her when she gave birth, the loss of a home confinement and the shock of giving birth in a cattle shed, the loss of having no home to call her own, having to be away from her home town for years, the loss of her husband, the loss of having no easy access to her son Jesus when he started his ministry, the agony of seeing her son tortured when he had done nothing wrong.

I wonder if she ever asked, 'What did I do to deserve this?' or, 'Why has this happened to me?' I don't think she did, because I believe that Mary was made with the ingredients to endure and to overcome, by the one who overcomes. Jesus said, 'In this world you will have trouble. But take heart! I have overcome the world' (John 16:33).

Jesus himself grieved. He was overcome with grief when he heard that John the Baptist was beheaded, and we're told that Jesus wept when he was at Lazarus's graveside – when he saw the grief of the crowd and of his friends Mary and Martha, he acknowledged their grief. He didn't say, 'Don't cry, never mind, I'm going to raise Lazarus from the dead.'

Jesus was separated from his Father when he was on the cross. At the time of his greatest need, in his final hours on the cross, he cried out, 'My God, my God, why have you forsaken me?' (Matthew 27:46). He alone can understand that cry of our heart in our own time of great need.

This is what Jesus does when we are grieving: when we weep, Jesus comes and weeps with us, he bears our sorrows.

Jesus said, 'Blessed are those who mourn, for they will be comforted' (Matthew 5:4). 'Who by?' we may ask. By the Holy Spirit, who is both the Comforter and the Counsellor. I know this to be true. It has happened to me and to countless others.

Even when he was on the cross enduring all that pain, Jesus thought of his mother and her grief and loss, and also of his friend John. He called to John, 'Here is your mother.' He was asking John to look after her. He called to Mary, his mother, 'Here is your son' (John 19:26–27). Later he appeared to the grieving disciples in the midst of their sorrow and mourning.

King David sinned, and when his child died he said, 'He can no longer be with me, but I can go where he is.' There can be a great comfort in this thought: in heaven we shall be with our loved ones. But what if they weren't Christians? Where will they be then? At the last minute, the thief on the cross acknowledged who Jesus was and Jesus said to him, 'Today you will be with me in paradise' (Luke 23:43). We can take comfort in that. Even if it's with someone's last breath, if they acknowledge who Jesus is, then they will be with him in paradise. It's something we'll never know for certain, but we can choose to let that person go.

The other day I was planting some winter pansies. They're so fragile, with spindly little stems that are almost transparent. I had to be careful not to break them as I put them into the ground. I suddenly realised that these frail little plants will live through rain, sleet, snow, ice and winds all through the winter, and their bright flowers will just keep coming and coming. This really amazed me, and I wondered how on earth they could endure all that battering. Then I realised that of course they can do it: they have been *made* to endure all the hardships and cruelties of winter. Just like us, really: we have been made to endure loss and grief. We have been made to bear the loss of things that have been snatched from us, our hopes and our dreams.

I remember someone who was talking about suffering saying that if God were to explain what suffering is all about to us, it would be like trying to explain physics to an ant!

When someone we love dies, we may realise that we never said goodbye to that person and it can cause us anguish. Sometimes we can even feel angry with the person who died, because they left us to cope alone. Pray to Jesus now and tell him that you want to say goodbye to that person. Express your sorrow to Jesus and ask him to tell the person how you feel. It may help at this moment to do something significant to symbolise saying goodbye. Maybe write a letter to the person and then burn it, or light a candle and blow it out while you say goodbye.

Sometimes people use a 'crutch' to help them in the grieving process. They might put flowers in a vase for a while, or visit the graveside or plant a special tree. After

Joanna drowned, I started to put two fresh flowers in a vase, two flowers for her two years of age. When it would have been her birthday, I increased the number of flowers. I did this for three years, until one day, when I was in the garden, I said out loud, 'I don't need flowers in a vase to remind me of you, Joanna,' and I went inside and threw away the flowers and had no need to do that any longer. It was helpful for a while, but then it almost became a super-stition – 'I mustn't let the flowers die, or. . .' Another thing I did for the first year was to visit the graveside, but then I realised that the grave was just full of the tent that Joanna had lived in, and she was no longer there. After that I only visited at birthdays and Christmas, and now I don't go at all. I let her go. We all need a crutch to help us along in dif-ferent ways. If you've never let yours go, I want to encour-age you to try it today.

Let's pray
Please come, Holy Spirit, my Comforter and Counsellor. I have kept hold of people, Lord, who are precious to me, but I want to let go of them to you now. I want to say goodbye now to . . .(name the person). *I choose to let him/her go now to you. Amen.*

See Jesus at the cross, or think of him there. Go to the cross and take with you the person to whom you want to say goodbye. Take that person's hand and put it into Jesus' hand. Turn around and walk away. Entrust that person to him.

Maybe we're angry at someone who died and left us to cope alone, or maybe we feel guilty. Lay it all down at the cross. Maybe we just need to weep and let Jesus weep with us. He is acquainted with grief and sorrow, he understands it, he has experienced it. Let him come and comfort you. He wants to.

SCRIPTURES

Though he brings grief, he will show compassion,
so great is his unfailing love. (Lamentations 3:32)

When you pass through the waters,
I will be with you. (Isaiah 43:2)

He will swallow up death for ever. (Isaiah 25:8)

The Sovereign LORD will wipe away the tears. . . (Isaiah 25:8)

Our Saviour, Christ Jesus, who has destroyed death. . . (2 Timothy 1:10)

There will be no more death or mourning or crying or pain. . . (Revelation 21:4)

* * *

Some people find it helpful to read a book about grief and loss. I would recommend the following:

Children and Bereavement by Wendy Duffy
Growing Through Loss and Grief by Althea Pearson
Living Through Loss by David Winter

10: Building Self-Worth

Over the last 25 years I've prayed with literally thousands of people carrying pain from the past, and I'd say that nearly all of them have had some issues relating to low self-esteem or self-worth. As soon as we're born, we look for unconditional love; we're made wanting and needing this kind of love. We have an unconditional-love-sized hole inside us and most of us didn't get it filled up when we were young. No parent can give it. It comes only from God.

If bad things happen to us at different stages of our development, such experiences can stunt our growth and affect our self-worth, our identity and our self-esteem. The perfect childhood would be to be born to two perfect, heterosexual parents, to live within a perfect family and go to a perfect school with perfect teachers. But life isn't like that!

Despite their best efforts, our parents often give us conditional love: it's based on so many rules and conditions. God's love is unconditional. His love is based on who he is, not on who we are! He's able to love us constantly and consistently regardless of our performance or attitude. We're often so used to receiving conditional love that we don't really believe that God can love us as we are.

We're going to look at these different areas, including our self-image and our identity in Christ. Let's look first of all at our self-image, the way that we see ourselves.

Look at the chart and tick those that apply to you.

1. A pessimistic outlook on life.
2. Lack of confidence socially.
3. Extreme sensitivity to the opinions of others.
4. A need for lots of structure.
5. A shifting of responsibility to others for unwanted or negative situations or feelings.
6. Perfectionist behaviour.
7. Self-consciousness about appearance or performance or status.
8. A striving to be a somebody instead of relaxing and enjoying who you are.
9. A habit of mentally going over past conversations or situations, wondering what the other people meant.
10. The same as above, but worrying if people misunderstood what you said.
11. Attitude of carrying a chip on your shoulder.
12. Inability to accept praise or a compliment.
13. Fear of intimacy in case it leads to rejection or a smothering relationship.
14. Fear of being alone.
15. Inability to express emotions.
16. Using negative labels in referring to yourself.

17. Worry that the worst will happen.
18. Self-defeating habits.
19. Defensive conversation and behaviour.
20. Critical or judgemental attitude to others.
21. Dependence on material possessions for security.
22. Sexual conquests to increase feelings of masculinity or femininity.
23. Habitually letting others walk on you.
24. Fear of God or thinking he is angry with you.

You may have ticked one or many. Don't worry about that, it just shows you the areas which you need to work on.

Let's pray

Jesus, I ask that you will show me in the months ahead more about the areas I've ticked; why I do what I do; and how I can change and receive your unconditional love. I surrender these ways to you now. Unravel them, Lord. I choose now to let you come into those areas of my life that need freedom. Show me a way through to a healthy self-image. Amen.

Self-image

This is like having a photo of yourself. Some of us think, 'If they really knew what I was like, they wouldn't like me.' The truth is that God does know what we're like and he likes us and he loves us. This doesn't mean that he isn't able to change us if we're willing for him to do so.

What we think we're like is portrayed in how we relate to other people, and it affects our response to situations around us. Maybe we had a difficult childhood and this has affected how we see ourselves.

The good news is that we can change. Do you have an old passport photograph? It seemed OK at the time, didn't it? But now, years later, you'll see that you've changed considerably.

After working on issues of self-worth or self-image, we can physically change our looks. What we feel on the inside is reflected in our faces and through our body language. In a crowd you can pick out the people who have a low self-image. You can tell by the way they dress, the way they stand, and even the way they hold their head. If you feel inside that you have an ugly face, then that's what you're reflecting. If you have a good self-image with the same face, then that image of yourself is reflected from your face.

Years ago, when I was 17, I worked with a guy who was really ugly. He had a huge nose, huge eyebrows, an unsymmetrical face and big lips. Nothing about him was particularly attractive, but after a few weeks I started to really fancy him. The reason was that he had such a fantastic self-image that he glowed with it. This was what was attractive – it made such a difference that his looks were enhanced by it.

A lot of things that happen to us from the moment of our conception can have a bearing on our self-image. Maybe we were illegitimate, or born as the result of a rape or incest. Or else we were born amongst violence or perversion, or maybe we were unplanned. This can all affect how we see ourselves. The truth is, our natural parents didn't give us life. God himself gave our life to us. He said that he wanted you, he wanted me, to be born. He is the one who breathes our spirit into us. Whatever circumstances we were born into, he can redeem us.

> The Spirit of God has made me;
>   the breath of the Almighty gives me life. (Job 33:4)

> And he is not served by human hands, as if he needed anything, because he himself gives all men life and breath and everything else. (Acts 17:25)

After birth we go through various development stages, in which we discover ourselves and the world around us.

From birth to six months

We have a body, spirit and soul. Our need is for nurture and care, to be fed, to be held, to be kept warm and to be prayed over. Our worth even at this age is stimulated by these things and they give us a sense of well-being. Some babies are left for long periods of time crying; for a baby this is its only way of communicating a need. If this becomes a habit, then it can affect a child's sense of self-worth.

Six months to 18 months

This is a time of exploring. At this age children aren't being naughty, they're exploring the world around them. Almost everything they find, they put into their mouth to taste, to feel and experience it. A parent with too much discipline at this age can really affect a child's self-worth.

Two years

At two years old we're learning from our mother and father what to do with our anger. We learn from our parents how they express it. We're looking for boundaries, as they make us feel safe and secure. This is a time when a child discovers what's allowed and what isn't allowed. Too much discipline before this can make us passive. If we have controlling parents, they will already have made their mark on us.

Three to four years

We're learning skills at this age, trying things out, asking a lot of questions. How that's handled affects our self-worth. At the age of three children frighten themselves with talk of monsters and scary things, as they're trying to discipline themselves to be obedient to their parents.

At four years old we can develop fear as a result of our parents' treatment of us. Between the ages of three and five our identity is formed: who we are, and who we are as male or female.

Five years

Five-year-olds have a great sense of right and wrong, and so it goes on throughout our childhood, passing through so many steps of development.

This would all be difficult enough if we grew up with two parents who loved each other. What if we grew up in a dysfunctional family, or a financially challenged family, with divorced parents, an alcoholic parent, a one-parent family, an absent parent, or parents who were not parented themselves?

There are some very good books written on child development relating to self-worth and self-esteem. One that I've read recently is *Healing the Past, Releasing Your Future* by Frank and Catherine Fabiano. Another book that I highly recommend is *Who Am I?* by Mary Pytches. This is full of exercises and teaching that promotes freedom and healing in the areas of self-worth and identity.

As we grow up, we can make judgements about ourselves and then live out of those judgements. Maybe others have judged us and we believe them and adopt what they say about us. Sometimes it's about the way we look or the clothes we choose to buy and wear. It has almost become a national obsession: clothes, image, to be seen to be going to the right place at the right time wearing the right thing with the right shape and weight! More and more people are having operations to change the way they look. In California, especially Los Angeles, women think it's a bit odd if you haven't had a boob job or a face lift by the time you're 35! Women in the USA are having false breasts, false bottoms and false lips, or skin lasered off, and it has now caught on here too in England. It isn't restricted to women now either: even more men are getting face reconstruction, as well as other parts of their body.

If we're tall, we want to be shorter, and if we're short, we want to be taller. If we have straight hair, we want it curly, and if we have curly hair, we use straighteners. If we're blonde, we want to be brunette, and if we're brunette, we want to be blonde.

We're never happy with our weight. Recently I was shocked to read that children – boys and girls – are now being diagnosed as anorexic at the age of eight.

People go to amazing lengths to reach what they feel are perfect looks. Some magazines are devoted to celebrities, showing photographs of them with cellulite and laughing at them. They then give them approving ticks if they're dressed correctly according to the editor's idea of what looks good. The world is obsessed with image. The media shouts, 'Look like this and you will have admiration! Drive this car and you will have acceptance!'

When I was 16, I was underweight at just over seven stone. I was asked by someone in the office where I worked if I had duck's disease. 'What do you mean?' I asked him. He replied, 'I bet when you step off the pavement your bum hits the kerb!' The whole office laughed, but I blushed bright red and went quiet. I was already self-conscious about my bum, even though I was only seven stone, and I thought this guy was referring to it. This is, in fact, a family trait: big bum, big hips and big thighs, coming down from my mother's side of the family. I felt so huge, and now I felt ridiculed. Years later, when I retold the story to my husband Ken, he said, 'No, he didn't mean your bum, he meant you have short legs like a duck.' What a shame he hadn't worked in my office when I was 16 – all those years of embarrassment for nothing! For years I felt so self-conscious about people walking behind me, thinking they were laughing at my bum.

Nowadays I think like this: God made me, he could have given me any size bum or hips or thighs he wanted to, but he, in his wisdom and delight, chose for me to have big ones. God doesn't make mistakes, so this must be what pleases him. After all, I'm made in his image. Who am I to argue with the Almighty? I now know that God loves big bums, big hips and big thighs. I've discovered that they do have their uses. Now that I weigh a whole lot more than seven stone, I've discovered that when sitting down I have my own built-in cushion, so I don't get a sore bum like some others do! I've chosen to change what I didn't like into assets. Big thighs keep me warm in the winter, and I have child-bearing hips!

Did anyone ever say anything to you about your appearance when you were young and impressionable? Did it hurt? Did you believe it?

Find a pen and some paper, and make a list of all the things you like about your appearance and then make a list of the parts you don't like. There must be at least three things on each list. I don't need to guess which list you did the fastest! Why don't you like those things about your appearance? Did someone say something about it? Do you have similar features to someone else in your family?

> For everything God created is good, and nothing is to be rejected if it is received with thanksgiving, because it is consecrated by the word of God and prayer. (1 Timothy 4:4–5)

Let's pray
Lord Jesus, I thank you for my body. I thank you that you made it different from anyone else's. Thank you that I'm unique. (Now think of a part of your body that you don't like and thank God for it.) *Jesus, you could have chosen it to be different, but you didn't. I confess now that I haven't loved what you made and I haven't loved this body you gave me. Sometimes I'm repulsed by it or hate it. I am so sorry, Jesus, please forgive me. Show me how I can love this body you gave me, Lord.*

LET THE HEALING BEGIN

(Maybe someone has caused you to hate your body because they abused it. If so, pray about this now.) *Jesus, come now with your cleansing and healing oil, pour it on my body and wash away every part that feels dirty; make me clean inside and out. I dedicate my body to you now. Show me how I can love what you made. Thank you that you were pleased with what you made.*

In your name, Jesus, I now accept . . . (mention parts of your body). *Thank you for the way you made me. I now accept that part of myself. Thank you that I was made in your image. Amen.*

Our self-image isn't just about what we look like, it's a judgement about ourselves. If our judgement is negative, then it's a judgement we need to confess to the Lord and give up (use the prayer above).

Now let's make a list about our judgements to do with our personality traits. Make one list of traits you do like and another list of those you don't like. Again, which is the easiest to do? We're often very negative about ourselves. Look at your negative list. Some of these things you can choose actively to work on and change; regarding others, you need to ask yourself the question, 'Why am I like that?' Look and see if some of the things are there because you learned them from your parents, or are you doing the opposite to what your parents did because you have a judgement against them?

How are you at accepting compliments? I used to be really bad at receiving them, even compliments about my own children. Friends would stop and look in the pram and say, 'Isn't she lovely!' and I would quickly reply with a negative, 'She's got terrible nappy rash!'

'Love your neighbour as yourself' is stated five times in the Bible and is listed by Jesus as the second greatest commandment. It's assumed in these verses that we love ourselves – self-love should be a normal Christian experience.

Husbands are to love their wives as their own bodies, and Scripture says that he who loves his wife loves himself, because after all, no one ever hated his own body. We see from this that we need to love ourselves, not hate ourselves. Get rid of hatred now in Jesus' name.

'What am I worth?' Ask yourself that question now and see what answers you come up with.

Mike Pilavachi tells a great story about a woman in Indonesia. I'm going to borrow it, because a lot of his stories are borrowed from someone else too! The story would obviously sound a lot better if Mike was telling it, with all his exaggerated facial expressions!

On an island off Indonesia there lived a man who was trying to find a wife. The going rate to buy a wife was three cows, but this man looked around and spotted a woman who wasn't good-looking at all. In fact, she had a face not dissimilar to one of the cows! The man went to the woman's father and said, 'I will give you five cows for your daughter's hand in marriage.' The father was overjoyed, as the going rate was only three cows and he realised that this daughter was the ugliest woman on the island. The man married the woman and she strutted about the island with her head held high. People all over the island couldn't work out why the man would pay so much for a wife, but the man knew what he was doing. He knew that all over the island people were pointing to his wife and saying, 'There goes a five-cow woman!' The woman also walked with pride because she knew what she was worth.

That's how it's supposed to be for us – not to be bought with cows, but to know that we were bought with a price, the greatest price that God could pay for us. Jesus did it because he thought we were worth saving. He came himself to die for us, to show us what we're worth. What am I worth? I'm worth dying for, and so are you! That's how I'm supposed to live this life: not just believing, but *knowing* that I'm worth dying for. That makes me feel very precious.

We're supposed to acquire self-worth as we grow up; it's supposed to be one of the building blocks of life. Some of us, however, either didn't get it or were robbed of it. This doesn't mean that Father God won't keep urging us to be like him, urging us to run to him to find our self-worth.

Another aspect of low self-worth is the feeling that you're a failure. We label ourselves as failures, and then wonder why we constantly fail. We're just being the self-fulfilling prophecy of our thought patterns; we're just living up to our label. In this area Father God intervenes with his love to help us through it.

Imagine a horse and its rider. The rider takes the horse up to a fence, the horse is afraid because the fence is too high, so he doesn't jump. What does the rider do? Does he give up? No! The rider encourages the horse to go up to the fence again, urging him on and encouraging him to jump. The rider isn't afraid. He knows that the horse can do the jump but is scared. Again the horse refuses to jump and the rider takes him around again to the beginning and lines him up to the fence. Once more the rider encourages the horse to jump, to fly over the fence, but the horse is still afraid and at the last minute doesn't jump. Again and again the rider keeps trying, until at last the horse sails over the fence and lands on the other side. The rider pats the horse and shows him his pleasure at conquering his fear. This is a bit like what God does for us. He believes we can do it – he thinks we're worth it, he thinks it's worthwhile to keep taking us to the fence. I love the verse that says, 'I can do all things through Christ who strengthens me' (Philippians 4:13), because he is more than able.

When our daughter was ten years old, I asked her what she valued; she replied, 'My blanket.' I asked her what it meant to her and she answered, 'Everything.' Then I asked her how much time she spent with it. 'As much time as possible, of course,' she replied. She was referring to what used to be a rainbow-coloured blanket that she had in her cot and pram when she was a baby, but since then it had become a comforter to her. It had been so loved and cherished and cuddled that it had become grey, devoid of all its colours. I was never allowed to wash the blanket. To me it smelled horrible, but to her the smell was one of the best things about it. I suppose in some way it was the thing in her life that never changed, it was constant, it was hers alone and it had been with her through every emotion, always held close. It had been smuggled out of the house on numerous occasions. As time went on and it became threadbare, she divided it into smaller bits so that it could travel more inconspicuously, especially to school. As she grew into a teenager, she even threatened to take her blanket down the aisle with her on her wedding day!

As the years went by, it became so old that only one piece remained.

One day, when she was 20 years old, I received a telephone call from Beth. She was in tears: the blanket had accidentally been flushed down the toilet! To be honest, her description of what had happened was so funny that it made me laugh at the other end of the phone, but I had to keep sounding sympathetic as I knew how much it meant to her. After we said our goodbyes and I clicked off the mobile, another call came through from Beth. This time she was begging me to ring someone up to look in the drains and if need be to dig up the road so that she could get her blanket back. With a smile, I chatted to her, saying that maybe now was the time to say goodbye to the blanket, especially as she was 20 years old! I explained that maybe Jesus was giving her the opportunity to say goodbye to it, and it was symbolic of growing up and saying goodbye to her childhood. That blanket was worth so much to Beth.

We are worth so much more than a blanket to God. He wants to spend eternity with us, that is his plan. He said, 'I am with you always, to the very end of the age.'

Have you ever seen the television programme *999*? Ordinary people rush to the aid of someone who is in acute danger, in danger of losing his or her life. Without any thought for their own safety, people jump into fast-flowing rivers, into fire, and battle through earthquakes and storms to rescue strangers. Without thinking about it, they lay down their life for those strangers.

Jesus did more than that; he was born to die. He knew what was coming, he knew that it would be a terrible death, full of suffering. He thought about what was going to happen, and he did it anyway. He *chose* to suffer and die, to be separated from his Father, to endure torture and shame. Why did he do it? He did it because he thought that you and I were worth it. Was he wrong? I don't think so.

Martin Luther said, 'God doesn't love us because we are valuable; we are valuable because God loves us.' The emphasis is on him, not us. It's because of who God is, not who we are.

Affirmation

Were you ever affirmed when you did your best? Or were you told, 'You could have done better'? How about when you failed? Were you made to feel a failure?

Years ago, at a conference, someone prayed for me and I fell down. While I was down on the floor, I couldn't open my eyes. Suddenly, flashing before me, were memories of all the times in my life when I'd felt a complete failure. For example, I was always last in any running races at school, and I could never get over the vaulting horse things in gym class. I tried my best, but I could never climb up the ropes. It was a big achievement just to get my feet off the floor! Another memory that came back to me in all its detail was the following.

During cookery lessons at school I always had to make apple pie, because my mum said we might not like anything else and it would be a waste of money! One week I was very excited as I was allowed to make a lemon meringue pie. As I got it out of the oven it smelled wonderful and looked great, unlike anything I'd ever seen before.

LET THE HEALING BEGIN

The meringue was a beautiful golden colour. I carefully lifted it out onto a wire cooling tray. Unfortunately, it must have been too close to the edge and as one of my classmates walked past the table, she knocked it off onto the floor. It smashed into lots of pieces and my hopes and dreams of taking something wonderful home were smashed just like that pie. I scraped what I could off the floor and wedged it back into the tin. When I reached home, my mum said, 'See, I told you it was best to make apple pie!'

As I now saw all these memories and felt all those feelings once again, I sobbed and sobbed. Failure after failure was shown to me; I felt so useless.

Then suddenly I saw them all again, but this time it was different. After each memory I heard Father God affirm me. He showed me again, running the race at sports day: 'Well done!' I heard him say. 'Well done for running your fastest.' Then I saw the climbing ropes and heard him say, 'Well done for not giving up. I saw that rope cutting into your hands. Well done, Jeannie.' Then the vaulting horse memory returned: 'Well done, I saw you trying again and again to get over that horse. Good try!' At last I saw the lemon meringue pie and my Father God – my Papa – said, 'I saw you make that pie, it looked and smelled so good. Well done.'

I continued to sob, but this time it was different. These were tears of joy and delight at being affirmed, something I'd never experienced before. My God brought me such a wonderful healing. He was there, he saw it all. I never had a mum or dad who came to see me do anything at school, so I never had anyone to tell me afterwards that what I'd done was good. But now God had done something that was life changing. This affirmation was hugely significant and was a turning point in my life.

Do you have memories where you need affirmation? Ask Jesus to come now and show you by the power of the Holy Spirit, and allow him to affirm you.

11: Discovering Our Identity

Who am I? If someone asks us, who do we say we are?

Have you ever been in a group of people and suddenly the leader of the group indicates that it would be rather good if everyone says a little bit about themselves? Most people hate it when they have to describe themselves or say something about who they are. It's interesting that mostly people say what their status is or what they like to eat!

Where do we get our identity and self-esteem from? Does it come from what we do as an occupation or what we spend most of our waking hours doing? Or does it come from somewhere deeper than that? As we grow up, we can hear a lot of negative words that we then take hold of as part of our identity. Did you ever hear any of the following words?

- You're no good.
- You'll never amount to much.
- You're stupid.

- You'll never get a job – who would employ you?
- Who do you think you are?
- Why don't you do as well as your brother/sister at school?
- You're incompetent.
- You're always seeking attention.
- You're not lovable.
- You can't do anything right.

Or did your siblings say to you any of the following things?

- You're not good enough.
- I can do better than you.
- I'm the favourite.
- You're too small.

At school did anyone say the following?

- You're a teacher's pet.
- You smell.
- You're ugly.
- You wear funny clothes.
- You're a four-eyes.
- You're different – you can't be in our gang.
- You're a freak.
- You must be gay.
- You could do better.

This barrage of negative words from so many different people in our lives can wear us down. If we receive a lot of these negative words and we don't know who we really are, then we won't have a sense of belonging. Then we'll not only start to believe what others say about us, but we'll take hold of these words as our identity. Sometimes just one or two things can take root, such as 'You'll never amount to much', and then other negative words just start to pile on top.

Part of my own identity was that I felt very inferior to everyone else. I grew up in Dagenham, where there was a grammar school for clever people and a secondary school for thick people. That was how I judged it, anyway. I wanted to go to the grammar school, mainly because my aunt, who is ten years older than me, went there. She would come to our house after school every day. I wanted to be like her and follow in her footsteps and I didn't know anyone else who went to the clever school. She was a role model for me. To get to the grammar school, I had to take the 11-plus exam. I'd taken all the exams except for the last one, which was English, my favourite subject. The problem was that on the day of the exam I was at home ill. I'd been in bed for a few weeks, and this was my first day being up and dressed – and my mum wouldn't let me go out of the house, let alone go to school. The headteacher came round in his car to take me to school, as he didn't want me to miss the exam. He said to my mum that he would have me back home again about an hour later. My mum refused to let me go. I was devastated by her decision, but no amount of pleading would change her mind. Naturally I failed my 11-plus, as I didn't complete the exams.

Months later, I was told that I could retake the whole lot. The problem this time was that my parents said it would be a waste of time even if I passed, as they couldn't afford the uniform and the other things that I'd need at the grammar school. This time I didn't even try to succeed; my passion to succeed had gone, and I felt beaten down. The retake results came and I was told that I was a borderline case and the board had decided that it would be better for me to go to the secondary school, where I could be near the top of the class, rather than go to the grammar school. Little did they know that I was the sort of person who flourished with a challenge, and my reports for the next few years indicated as much. For me this was a terrible blow, to end up going to the 'Dunce School'. I felt squashed, defeated and a complete failure. I believe that this was the start of my feelings of inferiority, which were simply affirmed as I grew up by all the other things that happened to me.

The 'Dunce School' was ridiculous. We only had one tennis racket, and no court. The only other sports equipment we had was a rounders bat and a netball! For three terms we didn't have a geography teacher, and not many teachers stayed for longer than one term. At the end of my education, the headmistress said to me, 'Can you see now what a waste of time it was learning all about history and geography? You'll never need it!' The only subject she was interested in was drama and elocution, in which she tried to get all the Essex kids to speak without a twang. Believe me, it didn't work!

This sense of inferiority affected me for years. I would be so frightened that people would speak about things I didn't understand. I would get what we called 'alien neck' – a bright red rash that started at the base of my neck and travelled up one side of my face. I often thought people were laughing at me or talking about me behind my back.

When my oldest daughter Alex was at senior school, I realised what a big influence teachers can have on the self-esteem of their pupils. The teacher would keep writing on Alex's written English workbook, 'Not bad.' How negative! Why write 'Not bad' when she could have written 'Good'? My daughter was put into lower and lower sets for English. Several terms later, she had a different English teacher. This sensible teacher wrote on Alex's work, 'Good try,' and, 'Progressing well.' This made such a positive difference. Alex started to go up set by set, until soon she was in the top one.

How interesting that she's now a primary teacher and one of her aims is to always build up children in their sense of worth by being positive about their endeavours. I was present one day in her classroom when she went through her daily routine of shaking the hand of every pupil in the class at the end of the day, with a little message of encouragement for each one of them. She explained later that this time was also an opportunity for those who had misbehaved to make their peace at the end of the day. Oh, how I wish this had happened in my school! What a difference there would have been for all of us.

'For as he thinks in his heart, so *is* he' (Proverbs 23:7 NKJV). Apart from negative statements, we can also have lies hurled at us. We can be taught that we're products of our past and we believe these lies and become like those lies. Unless that cycle is broken, we'll go on believing those lies. We can break free of those lies by coming against them in the name of Jesus and breaking the cycle.

Think of some of the lies that have been hurled at you and renounce them by saying, 'In Jesus' name, I say that the lie of . . . is not the truth.' And then state out loud the opposite of this lie: 'I declare the truth that . . . And I choose in Jesus' name to live in this truth now.' Start feeding on the truth, instead of feeding on the lies.

Have you taken any of the following as your identity?

- Inferiority
- Worthlessness
- Stupidity
- Failure
- Could do better
- Not as good as. . .
- Lazy like your father
- Bottom of the pile
- Attention seeker

If we can't accept the truth of who we really are instead of what others have told us we are, then we can't accept that anyone else could love us or accept us.

Let's pray

Lord Jesus, please forgive me for thinking that what I've accepted as my identity is how it must remain. I lay down now all the parts of my identity – of who I think I am – that have been fashioned by others. I choose to yield my identity to you now. Change my view of myself, so that I may be open to you, so that you can reveal to me who I really am. I want my identity to be in you. Show me not who I am, but whose I am. Amen.

I might not have had a good education, but that doesn't have to remain my identity. I can become educated whatever age I am and whatever my background, because the process of being educated lasts a lifetime. The whole of life is an education. This 'lack' will only stunt my growth if I allow it to.

> Make a careful exploration of who you are and the work you have been given, and then sink yourself into that. Don't be impressed with yourself. Don't compare yourself with others. Each of you must take responsibility for doing the creative best you can with your own life. (Galatians 6:4–5, *The Message*)

I can't go through life blaming others and my lack of education for my inferiority problems.

I never thought I would ever be able to do anything in my life that would be of any value. I vowed that I would never again set foot inside the hospital where our daughter Alex was born, as I'd had such an awful experience. Nonetheless, through God's grace, wisdom and – I have to say – sense of humour, he enabled me to be part of an initiative which meant that I ended up going to the hospital many times to relate to the midwives and nurses my own and others' experiences of having a stillborn baby. The result of this was that the hospital actually changed the procedure for dealing with bereaved parents. There were many other pioneering initiatives that were inspired by God, which the Lord used to build me up and encourage me in the belief that I did have something to offer to others – and which also healed areas of my self-esteem and identity.

We know the one whom the disciples many times called 'Teacher'. I need to find out who the Teacher says I am, so that I can identify with that instead of with all the negative rubbish that has been fed into me.

I used to think of myself as a blob on the pavement. Of course God didn't think of me as a blob, but the good news is that even if he did, he would still love me and choose me. It's not about what I can do, but about what he can do through me.

In Corinthians it says that God – that is, Almighty God – chose the weak and foolish things (the blobs, as I interpret it) in this world to shame the wise. He chose the things that are not (that are nothing) to nullify (to bring to nothing) the things that are (the things that are superior), so that no one can boast except for boasting in him.

I read these verses (1 Corinthians 1:27–29) when I was ill in bed after eating a dodgy burger, and the tears flowed down my face as I realised that God not only loved the blob I felt I was, but he actually chose me in spite of that. I sensed that he was telling me he could use me, but I really needed to let go of my opinion of myself so that he could show me what he thought of me. So I did, and I've never regretted it as I've grown in the knowledge of my identity in him.

So I will rejoice and celebrate that in the eyes of the world I may appear foolish at times, but my God loves me as I am, although he's always calling me on to grow in him.

One day I said to the Lord, 'I'm willing to be a fool for you. No longer will I live under man's judgement of who I am, or Satan's judgement of who I am.'

I realised that God had chosen a simple but faithful young girl to carry and give birth to his precious Son. He chose simple fishermen to be his first and closest friends. He called simple people to be his followers first. They

LET THE HEALING BEGIN

asked Jesus simple but foolish questions, such as, 'Can I sit at your right hand in heaven?' They often didn't understand what Jesus was telling them. They didn't even recognise Jesus when he was walking with them after he'd been raised from the dead! When he walked on the water towards them, they said, 'Is that you, Lord?' Who else did they know who did such miraculous things? God chose the weak and the foolish things of this world – he chose you and me.

The world says:

- You need status to be significant.
- You need lots of money to be important.
- You need to wear the right clothes to be a somebody.
- You need good looks to be successful.
- You need a slim, fit body to be acceptable.
- You need to be strong to survive.
- You need to have academic achievement to have something to say.

We have listened to the world and have agreed with it.

Satan whispers:

- You're ugly.
- You're worthless.
- You're insignificant.
- You're not worth knowing.
- You're not worth loving.
- You're not worthy to look Jesus in the eyes.
- You're a no-good Christian.

We have agreed with Satan and his lies for too long.

A prostitute kissed Jesus' feet and poured perfume on

them. Jesus said that what she had done would always be remembered and honoured. To a convicted thief he said, 'Today you will be with me in paradise.' Although Peter was impetuous and foolish at times, Jesus said to him that he would use him to build his church.

We need to start believing what we see written about in the Bible. We need to see the examples of the sorts of people God used to bring about his purposes.

> Long before he laid down earth's foundations, he had us in mind, had settled on us as the focus of his love . . . Long, long ago he decided to adopt us into his family through Jesus Christ. (What pleasure he took in planning this!) He wanted us to enter into the celebration of his lavish gift-giving by the hand of his beloved Son. (Ephesians 1:4–6, *The Message*)

Ask yourself, 'Is this truth or a lie?' Go with it, take hold of it, let the truth of it dwell in you richly.

Here is some more from Ephesians:

> It's in Christ that we find out who we are and what we are living for. Long before we first heard of Christ and got our hopes up, he had his eye on us, had designs on us for glorious living, part of the overall purpose he is working out in everything and everyone. (Ephesians 1:11–12, *The Message*)

Don't just read it; start proclaiming it as truth, feed on it.

Jesus said that if we abide in his word we are his disciples indeed. He said that we will know the truth and the truth will set us free.

I want to tell you my favourite joke – it's the only one I can ever remember! There was a great big lion and a little tiny mouse. The great big lion looked down at the tiny mouse and said, 'Why am I so big and strong and you are so small and weak?' The tiny little mouse looked up at the great big strong lion and said, 'I've been ill.' I love that joke, because that little tiny mouse has such a healthy self-image. He doesn't realise that he's little and inferior compared to the lion. All he knows is that he hasn't been well lately!

How do we have a healthy self-image? I realised that I was reading lots of stuff in the Bible, but I wasn't living the truth of it. Most of the time we don't grasp hold of Scripture and proclaim it as the truth. Doing this is such an empowering thing. Most of the time our thought life is feeding us negative things and lies about ourselves, so we need to counteract it with the truth. Sometimes we don't believe what we're reading, so we don't let it go inside us and feed us. The next stage is to start proclaiming it so that we get built up. Then it naturally occurs that we start to live out of that truth.

I decided that every day I would start proclaiming out loud some of the truths that I'd found written in the Bible. At first it just feels as if you're saying the words, but we're proclaiming it to ourselves, to the world and to Satan. I went through the New Testament writing out what the Bible says about who God is, and this is what I found:

- I am the light of the world.
- I am the good Shepherd.
- I am the Bread of Life.
- I am the Bridegroom.

Find out for yourself whole lists of what the Bible says about him. Then look at what the Bible says you are:

- I am the aroma of Christ.
- I am a child of God.
- I am complete in Christ.
- I am a temple of the Holy Spirit.
- I am God's building project.

Then I looked at who I am in relationship to Jesus:

- I am precious.
- I am his daughter.
- I am cherished.
- I am the beloved.

This, then, is my identity, not all that other rubbish. This is the truth that you and I need to live out of. Every day I declared these things that I was finding out. I was so full with them, I thought I was going to burst. Every time my thought patterns would tell me otherwise, I would draw an imaginary sword symbolic of the Word of God and shout out, 'No, this is the Word of God! This is who he says I am!' I hoped no one was looking through my window, as I would probably have been carted off to the nearest secure unit. This sounds like madness, but in those early days this was very empowering. Every day, if I was walking back from my daughter's school, I would declare out loud who Jesus was and who I was in him. After a while it was no longer just words, but powerful truth that was filling me up and flowing from me. I no longer just believed it – I had started living it.

We just have to say 'no' out loud to negative thoughts and tell all those thought patterns that we're not having this any more. Get someone to break and loose the power of negative words and the cycle and pattern of those words over you in Jesus' name. Ask Jesus for a sound mind able to receive and live the truth of his words.

My identity is in the one who made me and gave his life for me, the one with whom I will spend eternity. As I said at the beginning, I am a work in progress and I look forward to the day when I will be made whole.

Thank you, my Jesus, healer and lover of my soul. I will never stop thanking you for bringing me from death to life.

Come, Lord Jesus.

Further Reading

Here are some further helpful books. If these are out of print, they may be obtained on www.ebay.co.uk or www.amazon.co.uk, either new or second-hand.

Ché Ahn, *How to Pray for Healing* (Regal)

Dr Dan B. Allender, *The Wounded Heart* (NavPress)

Dr Dan B. Allender, *The Wounded Heart Workbook* (NavPress)

Rita Bennett, *How to Pray for Inner Healing* (Fleming H. Revell)

Andrew Comiskey, *Pursuing Sexual Wholeness* (Creation)

David Devenish, *Demolishing Strongholds* (Authentic)

Ronald Dunn, *When Heaven is Silent* (Authentic)

Frank and Catherine Fabiano, *Healing the Past, Releasing Your Future* (Sovereign World)

Canon Jim Glennon, *Your Healing is Within You* (Bridge)

R. T. Kendall, *Total Forgiveness* (Hodder)

Tom Marshall, *Healing from the Inside Out* (Sovereign World)

Floyd McClung, *The Father Heart of God* (Kingsway)

Russ Parker, *Free to Fail* (Triangle)

Leanne Payne, *The Broken Image* (Baker Book House)

Althea Pearson, *Growing through Loss and Grief* (Harper Collins)

Graham and Shirley Powell, *Christian Set Yourself Free* (New Wine Ministries)

Mary Pytches, *Who Am I?* (Kingdom Power Trust)

Mary Pytches, *Dying to Change* (Kingdom Power Trust)

Mary Pytches, *Yesterday's Child* (Hodder)

Agnes Sandford, *The Healing Light*

Jerry Sittser, *A Grace Disguised* (Zondervan)

Pamela Vredevelt, *Empty Arms* (Multnomah)

John White, *Eros Redeemed* (Eagle)

Charles L. Whitfield, *Healing the Child Within* (Health Communications)

Helena Wilkinson, *Beyond Chaotic Eating* (Roper Penberthy)

Pat Wynne Jones, *Children, Death and Bereavement* (Scripture Union)

Survivor Music

In Spirit and In Truth DVD: Soul Survivor Live 2006
Filmed at Soul Survivor 2006, this DVD captures the heart of a worshipping generation. At over 3 hours long, the DVD features the full length songs: Happy day, Love Came Down and Saviour, a 45 minute documentary, talks from Mike Pilavachi, Ali MacInnes & Andrew Croft and extended interviews with Tim Hughes, Lex Buckley, Mike Pilavachi & Rev. Graham Cray.

Love Came Down: Soul Survivor Live 2006
Tim Hughes together with worship leaders Ben Cantelon and Lex Buckley led worship at the 2006 event, where over 25,000 youth gathered for 15 days of worship, teaching and building community. This album is a major source of new worship material for churches with tracks including Happy Day, Through The Valley, Celebrate and The Highest & The Greatest. Also included is a bonus DVD featuring a 10 minute snapshot of the 2006 festival, as well as a preview of the Soul in the City vision for Durban in 2009.

We Must Go: Soul Survivor Live 2005
2005 saw another worship-filled 2 weeks at the Soul Survivor Festivals held at Shepton Mallet. As well as worship leaders Tim Hughes, Lex Buckley and Mark Beswick this year's album includes songs from Delirious? and Hillsong United. A bonus CD featuring live worship from Momentum: the Soul Survivor student and twenties event is also included. This features worship led by Johnny Parks, Martyn Layzell and Ben Cantelon making this an essential momento of the summer of 2005.

Dancing Generation: Soul Survivor Live 2000-2004
Each year over thousands of youth attend the Soul Survivor festival, where a highly anticipated album is recorded. Dancing Generation includes tracks from the best selling albums: Glimpses of Glory, Anthem of the Free, Your Name's Renown, The Message (live from Manchester) and Living Loud. Worship is led by Tim Hughes, Matt Redman, Martyn Layzell, Vicky Beeching and Mark Beswick. There is also a bonus CD which features ministry time music. These albums capture the amazing sound of a generation gathered to worship God.

www.survivor.co.uk

Survivor Music

Holding nothing Back: Tim Hughes

Holding Nothing Back is an explosion of energy, expressing a life of full-on worship to God. With tracks produced by Matt Bronleewe (Michael W Smith & Rebecca St James) and Nathan Nockels (When Silence Falls), the songs are epic and exciting. Tim is joined on guitar by Stu G of Delirious? and Lyle Workman (who plays with Sting), as well as Brooke Fraser (rising singer/songwriter from New Zealand) on guest vocals.

When Silence Falls: Tim Hughes

A great collection of songs from Tim, including strings recorded in Prague. When Silence Falls was recorded in Nashville, by Nathan Nockels (producer of Facedown and Chris Tomlin's latest), and mixed by Sam Gibson (who also mixed Delirious?' World Service). Tim Hughes' lyrics and melodies give you the freedom to sing not only celebrative songs but 'real life' worship songs. Including the songs: Beautiful One, Consuming Fire, Whole world in His hands and Name Above all Names.

Through the Valley: Lex Buckley

Lex has developed into a skilled worship leader and writer and has already contributed to the Soul Sista album Precious as well as Soul Survivor: Living Loud and We Must Go releases. Produced by Andrew Philip (Matt Redman's musical director & Soul Survivor producer) this emerge release from Lex features 7 great new songs.

Turn my Face: Martyn Layzell

Keeping his focus on congregational worship, Turn My Face is a new collection of worship songs which have a central focus of the cross. From 'The Passion of the Christ' inspired Turn My Face Again to I Stand In Awe, these songs will inspire the church in worship for years to come. Produced by Mike Busbee who also produced Martyn's debut album, Lost In Wonder, this promises to be a great resource of new worship songs for the church.

Lost in Wonder: Martyn Layzell

The debut solo album from Martyn Layzell: 'melodic, moving, intimate & inspiring'. Lost In Wonder made a real impact on the church. Its title song climbed the CCL charts both in the UK and in North America and the album won CBC Album Of The Year in 2004. Martyn has led worship on the main platforms at Soul Survivor, Momentum, Spring Harvest and New Wine.

www.survivor.co.uk

The Father's song & Where angels fear to tread: Matt Redman

The Father's Song: This album is less about catchy choruses and more about depth of relationship with God. Take the world but give me Jesus is a great slice of stadium rock. Elsewhere songs like You led me to the Cross and Thank You for the Blood reflect on salvation while The Father's song and Let my words be few have a naked simplicity to their fragile lyric.

Where angels fear to tread unveils a number of inspired new songs. Songs about the Cross, about God's mercy and about our friendship with God. Featuring the bonus track: Nothing but the blood with Tree63.

Facedown CD & DVD: Matt Redman

"When it comes to expressing our worship, what we do on the outside is a reflection of what's taking place on the inside. Facedown worship always begins as a posture of the heart. It's a person so desperate for the increase of Christ that they find themselves decreasing to the ground in an act of reverent submission." - Matt Redman

The album captures the live experience without losing the quality of Matt's studio albums. Featuring many new songs, including Worthy, You are Worthy (duet with Chris Tomlin). The Facedown DVD includes 12 songs of passionate, reverent worship. Including 3 talks from Louie Giglio, worship conversations with Matt Redman, Darlene Zschech, Graham Kendrick and 'Notes on songwriting' with Matt Redman, Beth Redman, Tim Hughes & Mike Pilavachi.

Facedown book: Matt Redman

"When we face up to the glory of God, we soon find ourselves facedown in worship". Matt Redman takes us on a journey into wonder, reverence and mystery - urging us to recover the "otherness" of God in our worship.

Passion for Your Name: Tim Hughes

Timely and timeless advice for today's worship leader. If you want to be more involved in leading worship in your church, or become a more effective member of the band, then this book is a great place to begin. Tim Hughes looks first at the reasons why we worship God, and why we need to get our hearts right with him, before moving on to the practicalities of choosing a song list, musical dynamics, small group worship, and the art of songwriting.

www.survivor.co.uk

Survivor books...receive as you read

Survivor Books came out of a desire to pass on revelation, knowledge, experience and lessons learnt by lead worshippers and teachers who minister to our generation.

We pray that you will be challenged, encouraged and inspired and receive as you read.

Worship, Evangelism, Justice:
Mike Pilavachi & Liza Hoeksma

We know that worship is much more than singing songs to God. Don't we? This book looks at what happens when we let *Worship* infuse all areas of our lives, what *Evangelism* looks like in today's culture, and what God's passion for *Justice* means in a broken and hurting world. God holds all three close to his heart: if we bring them back together, could we regain the lost voice of the church?

Wasteland: Mike Pilavachi

With honesty and wit, Mike helps us to understand - and even relish - those difficult times in our lives when our dreams are unrealised and our spirituality feels dry and lifeless. Drawing from characters in the Old and New Testament, he puts together a biblical survival kit for the journey so that hope shimmers on the horizon like a distant oasis.

The Truth will Set You Free: Beth Redman

With insight and humour, Beth helps young women to find God's answers to the big questions and struggles in their lives. Thousands of teenage girls have come to trust Beth Redman's powerful and relevant teaching through her packed seminars at Soul Survivor.

Worth Knowing: Ali Herbert

A book of wisdom by women, for women.
Candid, yet full of hope, fourteen women offer encouragement and wisdom on what it means to be a woman living out the Christian life today, alongside five powerful real-life stories of God at work in women's lives. Contributors include: Fiona Castle, Diane-Louise Jordan, Amy Orr-Ewing, Minu Westlake, Mary Pytches, Ali MacInnes & Rachel Hughes.

Survivor books...receive as you read

The Smile of God: Andy Hawthorne
You can't win God's favour - it's been won for you. But you can live in such a way that you know His smile on your life. If you're tired of conforming to the pattern of the me-centred world, if you're open to the disciplines and the passions of a real man or woman of God and if you're ready to trust God in times of discouragement or outright opposition....then let this book kick start, or fire you up again. God's smile awaits you.

God on Mute: Pete Greig
Writing out of the pain of his wife's fight for her life but also the wonder of watching the prayer movement they founded touch many lives, Pete Greig wrestles with the dark side of prayer and emerges with a hard-won message of hope, comfort and profound biblical insight for all who suffer in silence. Tracking Christ's own unanswered prayer through Gethsemane and Golgotha, the book leads the reader to Easter Sunday where miracles arise – often when we least expect it.

"If you are hurting and secretly wondering 'Where is God?' and 'Why's this happened to me?' and 'How come my prayers aren't working?' then I dedicate this book to you..." – Pete Greig

Incomparable: Andrew Wilson
God Most High. The Lord. I Am. YHWH. Father of our Lord Jesus Christ. Maker of heaven and earth. There can be no greater inspiration, no more solid ground for hope, no better source of comfort, no other reason for worship, no clearer light to steer by, and no stronger motivation to live well. Andrew Wilson explores 60 names and descriptions of the one true God, weaving profound biblical insight into each short chapter, and so unfolding the greatest subject our minds and hearts can ever contemplate.

www.survivor.co.uk